TENNIS SHENANIGANS

AND BOOYA SANDWICHES

Other undertakings soon to be available:

Carpie's Capers

Goodbye Edie
100 years of stories

The History of a Garage Band Journeyman
Hometown hero's journey Home
A true Artisan

Schwanengesang—'A Year to Say Goodbye'
Journal Excerpts—Some books will have a shortened version of this as a bonus

Archie's 'Second Helping'
His second wind to be second to none
Our first undefeated season, just like the Patriots

Roessler
My personal comedian

The don't be a dumb-ass policy is still in affect

Catch 22 turns into a Catch 23
Damned if you do—damned if you don't.
Relinquished to just coping with existence itself

Mike and Friends Reunion 'CD'
Music to jog by

Bette you'n me

Book of Murals
Attack of the 40-foot mural; Apprenticeship with a true Artist

TENNIS SHENANIGANS

AND BOOYA SANDWICHES

My stories are better than yours, Just sayin'

Pure unstepped-in Moral Scruples

Michael DiGiantommaso

authorHOUSE®

AuthorHouse™
1663 Liberty Drive
Bloomington, IN 47403
www.authorhouse.com
Phone: 1-800-839-8640

Illustrations and photographs, from the archives of the author.
Photographs by Mike or Laurie DiGiantommaso or a bystander we begged.
Arizona photographs used with permission from Cathy Haynes.

Some names and unimportant facts have been altered to protect the identities and pride of said friends and foe. Keeping friends, friends and keeping Foes out of the courtroom.

Published by AuthorHouse   04/23/2012

ISBN: 978-1-4685-4303-2 (sc)
ISBN: 978-1-4685-4302-5 (hc)
ISBN: 978-1-4685-4301-8 (e)

Library of Congress Control Number: 2012905470

This book is printed on acid-free paper.

Cover design:
The METAL 'T-2000.' The heaviest, most uncontrollable tennis racket ever invented. My first taste of tennis technology. It still has the original strings.

The public town park tennis courts; where legends were made and fantasies fulfilled. Two courts tucked in a sinkhole behind the General store of a quaint New England town. Run down from many years of neglect, but still a beautiful place to play, with hourly Church bells letting you know you've been there way too long. It tolls for thee. Lovingly referred to as the 'Hole.'

It was everybody's private tennis court.

Booya means = Hell yeah! In your face! It's also a tasty stew

I emerge to don the clothing of truth.

I would like to dedicate this book to my Wife:

Laurie Diane Henry DiGiantommaso

Partners in tennis, Partners in life.

With a special thanks for the invaluable help with the final drafts

I am grateful to those few people who read and commented on a few rough first drafts:

Karen and Tom Carpenter,—Honey (BB) Archibald,—Charles Durang, —Chuck Roessler,—John DeMeo,—Michael Chwalek,—Fran DiGiantommaso, —LDHD.

* Some descriptions of people may seem harsh at first.
I may have added a little extra humph to get certain impressions across. That was my first impression of them.
All victims have been warned. Friendships have followed and I have learned to love them all.
Sometimes knowing how others perceive you can be exciting.
Even if it isn't always flattering at first.

In the end—Foe became Friend.
With the Exception of Sir Bruce he is still a curmudgeon.

We all have a natural Defense against criticism—
We don't like it!

Cut out the Bullshenanigans

My stories are better than yours, Just sayin'

Any comments or suggestions are welcomed.
If it's about misspelling or punctuation, keep it to yourself,
your too late.
Mikedigiant@comcast.net

Karen Carpenter quotes:
(Harvard alumni—writing mentor)

There are hundreds of ways to write. All are good.
Just write . . . Keep it simple.
Don't worry about punctuation and you have permission to rewrite.
Don't write about the ice cream cone on the way home from an adventure.
Unless it was really, really good.

She whispered, "Your story was **powerful**." . . . (*What a wonderful word*)
"You have a voice and a style." . . . (*True inspiration*)

Tom added;
It's your emotional side making you write. Your feminine side poking out,
but you carry it really well on your stocky man-body. 'tee-hee'
I wouldn't be ashamed to show my feminine side, if I had one.

TABLE OF CONTENTS

Introduction

A compilation of short stories. 'Buddy stories' surrounding the battlefield of tennis.

These stories could have been taken from any sport; softball teams, dance competition, police academies, political campaigns even bingo or poker night. Any place people get together, play games, and compete. It's about people in pressure situations, tales with in-depth observations through relationships with friend and foe. Some friendships lasted years, some just a season, or a single tournament. Grudges lasted decades.

All have spectacular endings, some taking as much as ten years to wreak vengeance, or win the coveted token of victory. When I say great endings, I don't mean all happy-endings but exciting, with twists like only true life can dish out.

These observations will tickle the avid tennis player as well as anyone who deal with people in competitive situations. Battling the town, the league rival or your best friend . . .
The truth simply Is . . .

Erik the Barbarian:
The meanest loudest no nonsense, tell-it-like-it-is Drill Sgt. 'Tennis Instructor'. My one and only private lesson was an experience I'll never forget. This story gives him back the best compliment a student could give a teacher, and then some. 'He told me himself.' He has since semi-retired, and is writing his own book. Using this chapter in his book.

Gilligan's Wrath:
The worst partner on the face of the earth. He was a good tennis player and a nice guy, but on the court, he was *loud* and embarrassing, throwing racquets, degrading himself. No matter who threaten him, he could not stop. The incident that turned him towards Mr. Congeniality.

'Coming of age':
A teenager touring the Midwest in a 70's punk-rock band. Teaching tennis to kids on his time off—finding truth and the

'meaning of life' along the way. With an inner-body spirit cleansing, giving insight to why he is—who he is. (Top that Stephen King)

Secret Agent Man: *0007*   *Super* Heroes are real!

Covert operation gone wrong, captured behind enemy lines. In the meantime, his abandon: mother, dog and baseball cards come to live with me as he loses everything. His health, home, future-wife, and dignity slip away. Seven years later teaming up for a run at the local summer league championships, and a bid to re-enter society. It's time to collect!

Is there a Doctor in the house?

A July fourth weeklong tournament kicks-off with parades and fireworks, along with intensive cable and newspaper coverage. A disaster strikes and more than half of the players and spectators become hospitalized . . . Having so much invested they decide to pair-up the remaining players to continue the first day's festivities. When a couple of unlikely outsiders team up becoming the biggest news story in years.

My own personal Mt. Kilimanjaro adventure:

Our tennis team representing all of New England win a trip to play the best amateurs in the world. On our day off, we become sidetracked and lost. Hiking in the mountains after dark with a secret trail map looking for the tenth wonder of the world, the 'Devils ta ta' rock formation.

Lions, tigers and bears oh my. Do bears sit in the woods? Yes they do.

All stories are true. *Tennis etiquette and life morels to be learned and enjoyed. As you ponder the trials and tribulations of the characters, you get deeper insight into the author. He sees things from a slightly different angle than most. To the players it was just another game. To Mike it was a battle of life and death—Honor and Ego.*

If you've gotten this far I applaud you and realize I don't need to go on, . . . of course,—I continue . . .

The Hitman:

We played endless hours refining our games, but never had a meaningful conversation about anything outside of tennis. I didn't really care what he did off the court. *One day out of the blue, he vanished without a trace.*

A year later showing up on my doorstep. Was he in town to testify, before heading back to the witness protection program? Maybe I should have paid a little more attention.

My older brother:
He taught me tennis as a kid. Twenty years later we spent a summer together perfecting the real game before he passed that winter. We both regressed to our childhood sibling roles. I knew that court time with him was limited, and cherished every minute. I never expected murder.

The perfect kid:
Movie-star handsome, athletic, impeccable manners and work ethics. Doesn't drink, doesn't smoke, doesn't snack between meals. Their must be a catch. Nobody is this good. The adventures were perfectly implausible.

A Cock and Bull Tale:
Cockamamie myths and phobias. People are still people—some a little merrier than others. "Mike, your wife's on the phone."

The Rocket Scientist:
Diagnosed with terminal cancer. As we wept together he pondered how he would be remembered. The eulogy we wrote together became a tribute to him and became the basis for this book of misadventures.

Michael Chwalek inspired me to put down on paper all the funny stories we shared while I visited him in the Hospital. Encouraging me to finish this project, of course, in his honor.

First of all, he didn't want his golden tennis years to be lost in infamy.

He wanted them to be remembered in all their glory and reverence.

Ok, maybe there was just one reason but it was a good one.

Dangling the Carrot—Urging you to continue.

Basketballers

"Friendly Backyard Tennis Saves Mans Life"

(Dinka tennis to the Big Leagues) 'A little background to get started'

I basked in the glory of competition, playing all sports imaginable.

As I aged somewhat gracefully, I had to give up sports for one reason or another.

Basketball was the chosen game for me because as a kid, I could practice alone for hours. What a great stage for a high school guy to impress the ladies. Basketball gave me reason to stay in shape as I aged, but all too soon I had to give up that sport due to nagging injuries like: broken fingers, constant sprained ankles, and chronic back problems. Creeping into my forties, the healing process slowed down to a crawl. Putting ten guys together fighting for one ball was an injury waiting to happen, and happen, it did, over and over. With long-time friends retiring and younger punks thumping me the thrill of victory waned thin.

Tennis take-over

During the summers the basketball group would meet Sunday mornings at the town-park playground, keeping our brotherhood alive, and getting us out of house-chores.

One day someone brought a couple of tennis rackets as a joke for the guys waiting to sub back into the game. The next week most of the guys brought their own rackets and now the tables were turned. From then on, it was all tennis every weekend, with a basketball to occupy the sub.

Basketballers playing tennis is all fun and giggles until someone loses. Then the competitive juices start boiling. It was a fun new adventure that didn't breakdown my body, although it did wear out my sneakers.

A bunch of good athletes with wooden tennis rackets and old worn out balls. We didn't know you opened a new can every match. We were spin-doctors, slice and dicers, with great overheads, and push serves. Masters of close to-the-net dinka tennis with superb hand-eye coordination . . . Fun slow-paced tennis.

I was the one to get the tennis bug. Searching out tennis books and instruction video's and getting a super ($200.00 Wilson Hammer) racket for Christmas. The most expensive racket I had ever seen and I still had to buy strings for it. I would stand and stare at it every time we went to the Mall. I couldn't believe someone would pay that much. I had to have it. That alone would make me a *player*, well, that and some cool *hundred dollar Nike sneakers*.

An ad in the newspaper sealed the deal. *The local YMCA was giving cheap group tennis lessons*. To my surprise, my wife showed an interest so we decided to try it out together. What a concept, a married couple playing tennis together, and we were pretty good together. She even subbed-in with the basketballers a few times.

Before long, I was searching out better singles competition, players around my own level. We would play for endless hours. It didn't matter what the score was. The points were the drug . . . the rallies we couldn't get enough. All life problems faded away, like therapy. Giving up sports that you trained for and excelled in all your life given a new forum.

This of course led to local summer leagues. That, forced us to work harder to get to the next higher level. Then we found *inside* club tennis! We got tired of shoveling snow off the courts to play one more game before the season ended. Playing at a tennis club for us seemed out of reach. No one would pay that much for one hour of tennis. We had always played three or more hours at a time. I still have a bit of trouble with the cost, but you really can play hard and physically in an hour and get a good sweat going. I was entering the 'Tennis Zone'.

Renting courts late at night, (during the winter), because they were much cheaper, and they would let us play longer without paying extra. Sometimes playing until midnight. The club was happy with the new prospective members and the beer tab. All the die-hard tennis friends I had befriended, started to assemble with us. We were a squad of so-so players. We had up to four courts reserved every Thursday at nine pm.

The club caught on and formed us into a league and scheduled Thursday nights for us to play singles against each other, with a couple of hours to play real fun doubles after the games free . . . until closing!

This was great and cheap . . . and the club made out too. Membership was down at that time. The club over the next year added new players to the league, and change dates and times. Then cut out the after-game fun, and of course, hiked the price. It just became a league of people we didn't know. With the added weaker players, we needed something more to grow. It was time to search for new venues. That's when we found USTA!

As a group of guys who had never been rated. We all took the ratings test together and formed our first team . . . a USTA team. **Carpet Diem** was formed. What a great name for a team, we were geniuses. The 'Forecourt tennis Club' where we played was the only facility around that had a carpeted court surface. A unique experience playing on the slick surface of an indoor/outdoor rug placed over cement. A tremendous advantage to the home team that practiced on it. **Carpe** Diem, taken from a "Horace" poem, meaning, 'seize the day', or 'enjoy and make merry the day for tomorrow may not come.' **Carpet** Diem was mocked mostly for what was figured to be an error in spelling on our jerseys.

The first year was spent getting use to the competition. We even hired a teaching pro to work with the team to show us the ins and outs. He was a God to us. He had been to the 'mountain,' and he could show us the way. He told us we worked harder than any group he had ever taught in his 100 years of teaching.

Our second year we won the local USTA league, the next year we made it through the Rhode Island State districts. Winning all of Rhode Island.

Finally the next step, winning all of New England, and it was off to the Nationals in Arizona. Not bad for a bunch of (late in life) starters.

I didn't know how rare this scenario was. I never enjoyed the moments enough while they were happening. I am still searching to experience it all again.

There is life (sporting life) after high school football, baseball, and basketball, and I don't have to worry as much about injuries, (ok, maybe tennis elbow) and I can do it with my wife. What a concept.

It's been a while since those first YMCA group lessons. What a journey it's been. I still from time to time call out my old basketball buddies, to play a little Sunday morning "dinka tennis." Of course, I have to bring the rackets and balls, and every so often slip in a 100 mph serve to keep them honest, or is it just to see the look on their faces. You might not believe it, but those basketball-buddies of mine were really good tennis players. If any one of them decided to study the sport, or if they too had been bitten by the tennis bug they could easily have come along on my journey. I'm always amazed at their raw talent, the only time they play is when I drag them to the courts, and they still keep up with me.

Tennis did save my athletic life.

My revelations of tennis have evolved to satisfy many passions.

Overhead smashes feel better than volleyball spikes, or slam-dunks. Booya! Serving is like a picture throwing fastballs, sliders, curveballs, change-ups and the dreaded walk, (double faults.) Groundstroke winners are like base hits. The feeling of making a three-point basket is there, along with crossing the plate scoring the winning run. A hundred mile-an-hour Ace up the middle . . . 'priceless.'

All my favorite sports rolled into one game, but much more action, and fewer injuries. *With a reason to exercise in between matches.* Tennis so far is awesome. Would it have been even better if I started younger? Would I have been better off as a kid practicing my serves, (instead of free throws, and three pointers) at a game I control? Not having to depend on four other players and a screaming coach. You can't foul out, or be benched for a dire behind-the-back pass in tennis. Who knows?

"Tennis saved my sports life"—and possibly my waistline.

MY Big BROTHER RiCHiE

The end of our sibling rivalry

Big Brother is Watching

The big black cast iron wood-burning stove in the kitchen is the first thing that comes to mind. He spoke of it often as his sanctuary. The warmth engulfing him like the safety of the womb. As a kid, he would curl up beside it for hours, his face absorbing waves of warmth. The stove was his gools 1, 2, 3 (olly olly oxen free) his home-base, his safe haven from *It*. A warmth that penetrated his whole body toes to fingertips. Richard often imagined he was back there, to fight off any pain and confusion. He confided in me, telling me to put my mind in a safe-place. This worked even at the Dentist. He was annoyed that I would not reveal my safe-place.

Richard was my older brother, or so I thought all my preschool years.

Growing up as a kid whose real parents abandon him. Two days old they placed him on his Grandmother's kitchen table and left. Just a blanket and a kiss goodbye.

He had a good life with people who loved him, several uncles and surrogate Moms, and brothers, (like me.) He was the ultimate big brother to me. He could do anything and he would teach me it all. Ok, not everything, the birds and the bees he left to my Dad. That was an unspoken oath, between them. I may have gotten a raw deal there. All Dad told me was, "It's better to be safe than sorry." Where's all the juicy stuff? OK, not bad advice after all.

Back then being born out of wedlock was unspeakable, but being born of adultery was a sin. You became an outcast. This had to be hidden from society, but always right there on your mind when you woke up. Always the first thing you thought about so you could hide it. '**It**' was a part of your life . . . '**It**' never went away . . . You had to be ready at all times to deflect '**It**'.

Poor Richard, a smart little boy, with a photographic memory, was told to hide his intelligence don't raise your hand, don't be the center of attention (blend in) . . . NO SPORTS . . . The first thing the school would want is a permission-slip from the parents, (heaven forbid) they find out he lives with his grandmother, without a real mom and dad. Without official legal papers. Would they take him away and put him in an orphanage?

My grandmother welcomed baby Richie with open arms as one of her own. Meanwhile Richard's father tried to save his failing lucrative marriage, to no avail. Yes, Richard's father was forced to give up the good life, stripped of his wife's great wealth. In the following years before his demise, he moved in with his mistress, Richard's biological mother. They were dirt poor and could barely support their several new offspring in the backwoods of Vermont. No electricity, proper schooling or indoor plumbing. Richard was better off where he was . . . but always wondering what he was missing. What about his real blood brothers, would he have anything in common, would they be sportsmen and scholars? Would they **be** like him? Would they even like him?

They didn't . . . Jealousy most likely. He was an outcast to them too. They called him a pretty boy with all his fancy new clothes. He couldn't work a farm, shuck corn or drive a tractor; his hands were soft and white, lacking the stains of the earth. To them, he was a city boy far from the likes of them. *A boy without a country.* After a brief visit or two, there was no communication between them.

He was far from a city boy, and didn't mind hard work, but he didn't relate to them either. Dirty, smelly, hand-me-down clothing, matted unwashed hair. Hillbillies with poor slang vocabularies,—unlearned. Defecating at the first urge wherever they pleased. Wild animals, he thought,—they couldn't be siblings?

With us, he had it good!

Richards Aunt Edith (my grandmother) took over, and became his mother. She raised Richard as her own, with the help of her twelve-year-old daughter Franny, (she was in charge of the early morning wood stove for Richard). As the years traversed young Franny grew into a beautiful woman, fell in love, and married

'Patsy' the man of her dreams. Luckily, he made it back from the war in one piece, purchased a home in the suburbs' and gave birth to a wonderful bouncing boy and one sad little girl, 'the American Dream'. Richie spent a great deal of time with my sister and me, especially summers. He was by default my older brother.

'My Older Brother' *the Motivational Trash Talker*

He coached me in baseball, football and basketball. A *true perfectionist* and a hard worker; together that makes an awe-inspiring sportsman.

Yes, Richard taught me the importance of practice; repetition until it was second nature, and you didn't have to think about it. I wasn't so blessed with the athletic body or natural ability, but I made up for that with exercise and preparation. Prepare for the game off the court as well: footwork, endurance, strength, flexibility, even good eating habits.

Hard work got me through high school sports and gave me the confidence to excel in academia and social life . . .

(Tennis wasn't considered a manly sport back then). Boy was I wrong it would have been the perfect outlet for me. Better late than never to learn tennis.

Rich loved tennis legend Jimmy Connors . . . The fact that he also was left handed, his feistiness and determination, everything about him. Often emulating Connor's crowd participation antics whenever he did a great play or won a close game. He *was* Connors. I by default, had to be **Bjorn Borg***. Not bad if you liked skinny guys with girlie long hair, super tight shorts and the emotion of a robot. That, Richard reminded me of as much as possible. My first real slice of tennis trash-talk. Richard was a master trash-talker, but it was for motivation. If I got lazy or tired this would give me reason to fight. He always knew what buttons to push, not going too far, (most of the time.)

Motivational trash-talking may not have been the best idea, but it worked on me. I learned fast, however *my trash-talking* was not motivational, and it involved some pretty jazzy dance moves. I didn't win much back then, but when I did watch out. Payback was a bitch.

Capron Park—11 years old

When I was young, Richie and I would go to a park where you'd put quarters in the light stand (one giant pole with two enormous light bulbs,) and play tennis until you couldn't move . . . Neither of us were tennis players just good athletes with wood rackets. Hitting and running around using ping-pong swings and old balls that had long lost their fur. They had to kick us out so they could lock up for the night. So much fun.

Driving in his little red Austin Healey Sprite convertible. The oversized teardrop headlights sitting close together on the hood gave it a frog or bug-eyed effect with a rounded smiling front grill. No trunk door, the trunk access was behind the seat, making a perfect cubbyhole to squeeze *all* his sports equipment and sometimes me. No outside door handles so you had to reach into the car to open the doors, making it feel like a mini airplane. I did feel like we were flying when we put the rag top down, which was all the time. It always seemed we were driving too fast and every slight turn of the wheel would wrench you back into the seat. Seat belts; not an option. The memory of pulling into the dirt parking lot, whipping into an open space spinning the wheels to make the backend slide over perfectly into position. Digging out loose change off the car floor gathering enough for a few hours of light from the coin-operated light-bank and letting me keep any extra for soda or ice cream on the drive home.

My first memories of tennis were good.

I lost track of him for a while as he tried the wonders of adulthood.

Brothers reunited

In my late thirty's I started to play tennis again.

Basketball season was over but the group still got together for a few laughs and exercise at the town park playgrounds. (Not tennis players, but athletes).

Rich had recently moved just across from the town-park tennis courts.

I told him of our Sunday morning tennis shenanigans, the fun . . . How it reminded me of the games we played as a kid, maybe he could join us. He did, and loved the competition. He fit in instantly as one of the better players there, even though the oldest by far.

He took it seriously. The excitement of mastering a new game, no more just pushing the ball around for him.

Time to hone new skills. We soon became hitting partners, and students of the game. Playing and practicing several times a week. We bought better rackets, and became tennis players. I brought the video camera and let it roll . . . We had fun more fun than I ever could have imagined. Not just tennis but I was playing with my big brother, and he was liking me.

Studying the game . . . He made it an obsession. He was not just gifted he would search for all the advantages, (like serving lefty, and forehands both righty and lefty (true ambidextrous). He used it to the max . . . he could even serve hard righty if the sun was a problem, or he just wanted to throw in a different spin at you.

The only thing that held him back from beating me was bad knees. He had just turned 50 and had broken or torn everything in both legs at one time or another. This was to my advantage, and boy did I use it. This was payback time for losing all those games as a kid, time to use the motivational trash-talkin' he'd laid on me . . . although I could never enjoy it for long. I hated to see him down. He pouted and stalled, and threatened to quit. He hated more than anything to lose. This time he didn't have the resources to train and practice to catch up to me, and had to give me my due. We next became partners and fought the world together as a team. We even entered a local tournament. This was a dream come true.

I had an edited video I made from recording several of our matches. We were pretty good and we laughed and giggled our way around the court. All the trash-talking and full antics caught on tape. I pulled out the best plays from both of us, adding Andre Agassi and Jimmy Connors inserts and made us look like superstars. I proudly brought it to him to watch together. He was out of commission at the time with a bad case of gout . . . It seemed like the perfect time. He was so irritated with me, he barked and threw it back at me . . . "Are you trying to make me feel worse?" He never saw the video . . . He would have loved it. I did.

We took the winter off from tennis. The following spring his health waned, nagging injuries, the gout and arthritis, etc . . . I sought out new players and started learning at an amazing pace. He grew sicker, I thought it was age, (but I am now the age he was then) and I am still a strong tennis player competing with all newcomers.

I expected him to get better, he was in his fifties not seventies. He did get a little better but not good enough to play tennis, and absolutely never wanted to see the video.

I still have the tennis video I made for us.

I loved making it, listening to our banter, his laughing (he giggled while he ran) he was having fun. That, made me happy.

The video was great. He would have loved it if he gave it the once over.

Maybe when we were old men sitting down for a card game, in front of the fireplace reminiscing, I could have brought it out, and giggled along with it. I have to find that tape right now, and . . .

Life became a death sentence to him. He wasn't the super athlete anymore, failed marriage, no children, no future conquests, or goals. He became destitute. He became a sour old man in his fifties. A great man never to receive his *just rewards*. With his skills and intelligence, he could have been the best at anything he tried. He enjoyed his life but didn't enjoy his old age, his body breaking down. His accomplishments never seemed to be enough. One of his mantras was, "Your only as good as your last game." Always looking ahead to the next big acquisition.

He had been a stone setter (rings mostly) as you can imagine the best around. He prided himself on quality not only the best work but the sheer volume was out of this world. Ultimately developing carpal tunnel syndrome and arthritis, wearing out his hands from years of sport and work. He was at a point that he needed drugs just to sit and work with his hands at all.

Therefore, he decided to go back to college to master Gemology, stone-cutting and buying. A new boundary to conquer.

Passing his college courses with flying colors and top honors, in record time, of course. He studied every chance he could. It had become an obsession no doubt.

Wanting to form a small business in his two level four-car garage, he called me, to renovate it into a small factory. He had some inheritance money and some borrowed money to start it up. He had a brilliant plan . . . and then he could let the cash roll on in. He would be the boss and teach, and give his hands a much-needed rest. He was recruiting me, promising riches and security. Imagine me working with my perfectionist brother. I gave it some thought.

During the process, he got an idea to double his business capital. He was close to genius but a little too close to be able to see the pitfalls of his schemes. (Gambling). Richard was a great card player; he had always been fascinated with the idea of being a high roller. He studied it and was pretty good at low-stakes gambling. Why not do it with high-stakes and double his investment. Moreover, he did win some, which gave him the courage to forge on. Vegas was calling to him and his photographic memory.

He lost every cent he had, and adding more to his problems, he went deeper into credit debt. Killing any chance of starting his own business and pegged him a failure to himself. This brought back all his anxieties and made him so depressed he laid down and never woke up. Died in his sleep. The cause-of-death certificate was listed—unknown. Murder? Suicide? Case open!

That phone call haunts me to this day. I did not want to see his corpse . . . My body wouldn't move. I forced myself into the car, scared. Was it really happening? I had to go to my safe place (in my mind), and Richie was there with me, helping me through it. I envisioned us on the tennis court. How good it was to be with my brother. It might not have worked at the Dentist office, but it worked here.

I just had an epiphany an awakening

Richard came to me in my sleep the night he passed, (not a premonition) a sort of goodbye. I can't seem to remember the moment, I told no one. I couldn't without breaking down; I still have the feeling come over me as I type. It was so real, as I drove to his home that dreadful morning, I remember wanting to share it with my mother. It was calming yet abstract. His body was still in his bed, up the stairs first door on the left. I plodded into the house, greeted with the announcement that my niece saw him in her dream that night. They all seemed at peace even calmed about it . . . I kept to myself . . . I am trying with all my might to remember. How could I not have this memory right up front and center? I have the feeling the emotional impact of serenity, but not the actual dream. Gone, for the moment.

I never told my wife. How could that be possible, I had to have told you?

I do remember! How could I have forgotten? Yes! I do remember.

I was elated, euphoric I have to tell my wife right away but I can't, the words wouldn't come out, as I choked up. I couldn't even get the first words out; to let her know I remembered. . . . That's why she didn't know. It was that damn video of me and Rich playing tennis.

The morning I was actually awakened with the bad news. I thought, "It couldn't be true I was just with him." Still groggy from being pulled out of a deep fulfilling slumber.

In the dream, he had invited me over. He was feeling better. We were watching the video, just as I had imagined, laughing and giggling. It was so satisfying; he had finally watched it and saw just how good we were. He was much younger in the dream, and didn't walk with a limp. He complimented me and ridiculed his poor form, stressing he would mend it now that he felt better. I wonder if he did come to me to smooth over our little conflict. We had not talked much since that day, not like brothers.

I wanted him to see how good we were. When you cut-out all the bad plays, we were superstars. I know there was more to it, I sense it but I don't feel that abysmal hole in my gut. No—in my heart. I believe we did watch the video together. He did see it. It was real to me. Who's to say what is real, if it is an actual memory with all the emotional baggage attached?

Tennis was the thing that had brought us back together for one summer. Time for just us two. Matching wits, learning 'the game,' sharing and enjoying the experience together.

I cherished that time and soaked up every moment, as if I knew it was the last. I never let on for fear he wouldn't play anymore. I knew my time was limited but never expected death.

I had him for that summer; we were so close for that short moment in time.

That summer he had invited me to Virginia to help a relative. We spent three days together, mostly cleaning, but on a moment off we went to an amusement park. Can you believe that! It was as if, we were back in time. I had his attention (all of it) just like a time-warp. We were kids again; I have the pictures to prove it.

We brought our rackets on the plane, hoping to hit a few tennis balls in DC, but never had the chance to play . . . Except in the airport, during a short delay changing flights, he took out an old ball and we started to volley, seated among the other passengers; no one seemed to mind. At least I didn't notice, while my big brother was giving me attention.

I will savor every moment.

"Leo the Lionhearted"

"The Best Thing **Tennis** has ever done for me"

'Sports Bully'

I played many sports in my day, and I felt I was pretty good at them all. Softball was a passion of mine from the start. Imagine the picture, throwing an over-sized ball underhand, slow with an arc. That's a slugger's dream. I was good but not the best, there was always one better guy that followed me everywhere and in every sport I played.

He was a bully to everyone around him—and he was always around me. I don't want to embarrass him by telling you his real name. For this article, we'll just call him 'Leo'. He was a few years younger than me, faster, stronger, and had the tenacity of a mountain lion. Yes, all the guys loved him because he made the team better, even though he was a sports bully. A pretty good guy away from sports but on the field he never thought anyone else was trying hard enough, and he let you know it. He would constantly bark, "MOVE YOUR FEET!"

Of course, he was the shortstop, to me being his sidekick third baseman.

The old saying, "Guys wanted to be him and girls wanted to be with him fit perfectly".

Bully was not even close to what he was. If I hit a triple he would have to hit a home run, even if he had to run-out an inside-the-park home run. He had to be top dog. We played well together, although he might not tell you that. Playing softball spring through frost bite, and then we would play basketball.

Did I mention stronger, younger, faster, with a desire like I only imagine pros like Larry Bird, and Michael Jordan would have. He was even better at trash talking. We had poker-night card games, ping-pong, competitive league volleyball, even darts. He always managed to be a little better in everything, and he continually let me know it.

We even started a side landscape business together, talk about competition. Who could mow the fastest, plant seeds, trim hedges, or dig holes better?

This didn't last too long. He tricked me into finishing jobs while he went off for more important things, (I told you he was smart.) It was destined to fail as we clashed on everything, especially who was paid more, for less work.—

All this until someone invited him to our Sunday morning 'dinka tennis,' with my basketball buddies. He loved the challenge and immediately was superior to everyone, just from his athletic ability alone. He learned fast. He, of course, wanted to play me at singles that day so he could single me out for another "Leo-whoopin."

However, (as you probably figured out) there was one difference with tennis. I Won! Finally, the old man could reverse the curse.

He became obsessed with the game, he couldn't stand being second best at anything; that made him a loser in his mind.

Yes, he was a tremendous athlete and super-smart. (Did I mention that?) But he could never beat me at tennis not even close. After a few weeks of beat-downs he whimpered, "If you didn't have that big serve, I would kick your butt"! From that day forward, I only served underhand to him. The beat downs were so much sweeter that way. I could taunt and laugh like he always did to me. I would shout, *"Move your feet!"* just to piss him off. Once I believe his head actually Imploded. It gave me such an incentive to improve my game and to work on my trash-talking. I loved tennis so much more these days. I had to work harder just to stay one step ahead of him.

I think he has a renewed respect for me. Wishful thinking? Well, more than 10 years later and he can barely win a single game from me, never a chance at a set. I have since given up basketball and baseball so he only has tennis left if he wants a chance to bully me anymore.

Sad to say he moved away so I don't see him but maybe once a summer when he comes back to visit relatives, and yes, we might play a little tennis for old time sake . . . but I will never let him win, even if we have to battle in wheelchairs.

Yes, I can trash-talk, I learned from the best!

Tennis has given me a lot to be thankful for through the years. With many stories to tell about tennis friends, foes.

Giving "LEO the Bully," a <u>beat-down</u> has to be "**The best thing tennis has ever done for me.**"

Leo I hope you get to read this . . .

I bet you're fat, and outta shape, at least I hope so. Not as smart as you thought, huh! So humbling isn't it! It's just about that time of year I usually hear from you. Brush off the dust and let's get it on!

Booyeah!

Jeez, I hope I haven't become a Sports-Bully. Hell yeah!

(Believe it or not Leo and I were very close friends.)

I would have been the best man, at his wedding, but he filled that roll himself, along with usher, photographer and baking the cake.

BOOYA!

I recently facebooked Leo, asking permission to use his name. After quickly giving me consent, he inquired about his chapter storyline.

A little flustered, he accused me of being too competitive. "Did you mention you took lessons," he asked in his defense? He paused—Then blurted, "I'm gonna write a better book and your not going to be in it—Booya"!

$\mathcal{S}ir\ \mathcal{B}ruce$ of Ecclesiastica

'Vengeance is best served cold,' with a side of biscuits.

I had not played in a real tennis tournament yet.

My friend Chuck worked at a State School for the mentally handicapped. Every year they raised money, with a charity golf and tennis tournament, and silent auction. He had gotten free tickets from a raffle he entered and gave them to me, ($150.00 worth). He was working at the event so he didn't need tickets.

The event was at a high-end golf course resort in Blue Hills just this side of Boston.

A very highly publicized fundraiser run by ex-Patriot, John "Hog" Hannah and former Red sox players. It was highly visible for big corporations to donate money and just send company workers to fill out the rosters.

This was a day-long event with gift bags, from local establishments. Several local businesses that wanted advertisement and charity write offs gave: skin creams, deodorants, soda, trinkets, gift certificates etc . . .

The day ended with a huge dinner and speeches from athletes, dignitaries, even the mayor, followed by the award ceremonies for the day's winners and a silent auction with some of the coolest sports paraphernalia: autographed items, signed footballs, baseballs, Jerseys, and even sailboat rides.

The tennis started off with a group lesson from the club pro, and the fastest-serve contest. Playing along with pro football and basketball stars like Tim Fox and Dave Cowens, and Mosi TaTupu . . . to name a few.

I did very well, and had high honors finishing third over all, with enough points to win my choice of ten new state-of-the-art Wilson tennis rackets.

This was a great confidence booster. Tennis all day, meeting several tennis players from the area and being complimented, and showered with gifts. *This tennis thing was all right.* I must be pretty good.

A week later I entered my first real Tournament—

I joined without a care in the world; let's see what I can do. I won my first two rounds of singles, fighting with all my might. I thought these were great players; the mental stress was as grueling as the running.

I kept telling myself it didn't matter if I lost, this was just a test for the fun of it.

My next opponent was *Sir Bruce*. I had overnight to prepare. I was telling a tennis friend about my success and he told me, "Bruce had won this tournament a few years ago you don't stand a chance." You can't compete. I told him of the new racket I had won last week. He laughed, "That was a fluke, they give out tons of free shit." "You didn't win the tournament. You placed in the top 10 of an entertainment folly."

With mixed emotions, I reluctantly went to my doom.

Sir Bruce was tall and lanky, 'regal' is the perfect word, (snobbish is right up there too).

The warm-up was tough, I didn't know there was a warm-up routine. I wasn't good enough to control the ball to go right to him especially when he was hitting fairly hard at me.

We were on the show court, and the bleachers were full. I was in the main event! Yikes! I felt so out of place, so naked.

Bruce came on strong. He was by far the best player I had ever played to date. I was barely able to scrape a few game wins for myself. What could I possible do to beat this guy? I bet he could give Agassi a run for his money. He volleyed a ball that just died—it hit the ground and didn't bounce. I had never seen anything like that! When I complimented him, he snarled and turned away.

I lost, but I played pretty well considering, and I won four games. It wasn't a romp, and he had to work really hard. I was exhausted, but I was proud enough. I was photographed and interviewed by the local newspaper. Wow! . . . I had said nice things about all, and congratulated the director on a fine tournament etc . . .

A fairly good moment, no a great moment.

I saw them go over to Bruce I couldn't really hear what was going on, but he looked a bit frazzled as he spoke, complaining about the hot weather, the bad courts, the time he had to play etc . . . I didn't hear too much, but I was surprised of his complaining since he'd won.

That next night reading the article I was in ecstasy, there I was a tiny photo in the upper corner on the *front* page looking good smashing a forehand. My little write up under the photo was edited down to a few choice words, not bad.

I opened to page two and there was a full-size behemoth photo of Sir-Bruce standing next to the interviewer. Towel around his neck sweating profusely, mouth open, sternly discussing the match. Bruce was mad; he was mad with his draw, his seeding, his scheduling, everything. He was getting a raw deal. Why did he have to play me? (a nobody) . . . He should have had a bye until the final rounds. I wasn't even in his class. He only lost a few games when it didn't count, he had already been ahead winning easily. What? I was devastated, he made me out to be a buffoon. I shouldn't even be playing. Why would he say that?

Why would the interviewer write it? This was uncalled for. I had an immediate hate for him after I got over the pain, and agony of being a nothing. I was totally embarrassed. What would my friends think? I was not a great player I didn't do things perfect yet, I was just learning what a tournament was. Why was he so mean? Was he embarrassed to have lost those few games? Did I make him look bad with my strange play, junk-ball hitting and running down balls? It took a lot of effort and about two hours in the heat for him to beat me. He was, mister-prim-and-proper, trained at the finest clubs, by the best teaching pros.

Bruce was a smudge. A bad mark on the face of tennis. This has stayed with me for years, even the mention of his name gives me shudders.

I saw him in a sports store one time and walked right up to him, looked him in the eye and told him, he nearly squashed my attempt to learn tennis. So what if I wasn't great, I always give my opponent credit for trying. Have some gall and decency. Treat opponents with respect, if you're better, more power to you. Why would you say, I was just lucky to win a few games when it didn't matter?

Bruce just said, "Do I know you?" He probably get's this all the time, as he walked away.

I think that's what I said to him. I was pretty nervous. Still I have no satisfaction. This was a reoccurring nightmare; I'm not so sure it actually happened.

This could be the reason I always went to the underdogs defense, took them under my wing and I always complimented my weaker opponents. Most of them anyway.

The rematch'—Wheaton College

<u>Many years later</u> a local College was having a fund raising tournament and I had the chance to play Bruce once again. Only this time it was doubles and I had a worthy partner. I had been playing for quite sometime now; I had even been to the Nationals. I was tournament tough . . . a veteran tennis warrior. *Maybe eight years later.*

The participant roster was small only five teams. I'm sure Bruce didn't recognize me from Adam. I was a nobody to him.

Late October, playing inside a field house at Wheaton College.

The court surface was a rubber they called 'cork', with a racetrack running around the outer edge, and drapes of vinyl hanging from the ceiling, separating the courts. On the rubbery surface, slice was deadly as was a kick serve—both my specialty. I was primed for retribution, my comeuppance.

Nobody was watching no spectators not even the tournament directors, just a few runners stretching, and jogging around the outer edge.

It was a round-robin format given the odd number of teams. We played each team once with a shorten match—(nine game pro set

NO ads). A quick game but still pretty fair. A good format if you're playing four matches in one day. Approximately 30 minutes each match.

The two best teams were to play for the trophy the following Sunday morning.

We played Bruce first.

I was hyper, breathing hard trying to get oxygen to my brain,—feeling faint. I had explained the ordeal to my partner Alfredo. I suggested we slam everything right at him and hope for the better, "No, let's play our game, we are good," Alfredo said, with a cool 'Antonio Banderas' accent.

I warmed up with Sir Bruce, hitting hard firm shots at him, showing him I was a seasoned player now. Each return I would hit a little harder adding a little more spin, backing him deep past the baseline. He didn't falter or even flinch. I put extra effort into my overhead practice, slamming rockets right at him. He remained stoic.

Finally the game was afoot.

My partner let me down, having the worst time with the environment and the cork floor. He had big loopy swings and found it difficult to get a full cut. It was over in an instant.

We should have made a better debut, but Alfredo sucked and I tried to make up for it, sucking even worse resorting to plan 'B', (smashing everything at Bruce). Not a good strategy. I should have known.—*Was it too late to get another partner?* Well, that surely gives Bruce ammo for the newspapers.

But this was not over yet.

Funny enough from then on the pressure was off Alfredo, as he adjusted to the court. Now I remember why I ask him to be my partner. We next played a much weaker team. Flogging them **and the last two remaining teams.** That gave us confidence as we made it to the finals. Again no one seemed to care. We had to find the director to tell her we had finished; even she had better things to do.

We were scheduled to play Bruce's team the next morning early at 7 am for the "Indoor Tournament Title."

Having to start extra early because they had a track-meet scheduled at noon. I always had a hard time playing in the early morning because of back spasms, so I had to get up extra early and workout, mostly treadmill and stretching. *I was willing . . .*

A regular best-of-three-sets match to push forth a new Champion.

Bruce thought we were insignificant, not worthy of his attention. He had good reason. He saw us play. He demanded the trophy; they had won **all** their round-robin matches, including us. He felt that was enough.

Why does he have to play us again? That's a waste of his Sunday morning. Was he going to miss Church? Like he was the church going type.

I remember he was late, nearly 40 minutes late and I was hoping for a default. Looks like it's an 8 am start now. It seems He had called ahead with some lame excuse. This was more of a bother to him.

GAME OVER! WE WON!! Yes—WE WON!

Alfredo was incredible in our rise to victory. That much I recall.

I honestly don't remember the game, I don't believe it was a close score, nothing stands out. Did we even shake hands? I would love to shake his hand hard and firm, not letting go right away, looking him in the eye, rubbing in my victory.

The director handed us mugs, no confetti, no pomp. I looked at the so called trophy 'Mug' thinking, "Did they get this from the teacher's lounge, where's the trophy?" It was just a regular white coffee cup, with a tiny gold sticker that read, 'Wheaton College Tennis.'

. . . . I'll take it gladly, at that point I didn't care if it was the janitor's old school keychain. Yes! We won! Vengeance is sweeeeet!

I finally had my chance for a speech though, only five people would hear it . . . Just for Bruce?

Wait! My speech, it would have to be quick as he gathered his gear and rushed off, probably to catch the last sermon, L.O.L.—*Charlie (his partner)* and Alfredo bolted as well.

I asked if she was going to put something about our victory in the newspaper. There was always an article. This would be the same newspaper Bruce battered me in, it circulated through several towns.

Bruce was a local tennis icon, mostly for those that hadn't had the pleasure of his company. She grabbed her clipboard as I made my speech-interview.

I started, . . . Bruce and *Charlie* (I don't remember his real name) were worthy opponents, but on this day in October the day of our lord, they couldn't compete with destiny. Bruce had scorned me many years ago when I first started out and now my revenge is complete. Bruce it's time you hung up your tennis sneakers. Because when you lose to someone insignificant as me, you become insignificant. I schmoozed on and on . . . but that was the jest of it. Pretty close I would say. Athletic Director (Lynn) promised she was going to submit it that very day, with a slightly edited version. I told her this would make everything better; as I explain my fairy tale of poor sportsmanship and misery.

I couldn't wait for the paper the next day. . . . Nothing . . . Tuesday's edition nothing. I called; she assured me it was coming. Wednesday's sports edition, finally, I went through and didn't find it. I scanned several times as I came across two lines buried in **the local sports news** section.

It READ:

Sir Bruce and Charlie Such-n-such lose for the first time in five years . . . Their reign of dominance comes to an end. Sir Bruce had won this fall classic seven out of the last ten years . . . Well, There's always next year?

What?—The editor must have been a fan or a father. Talk about let downs. I wasn't even mentioned . . . **Well, at least I have my Mug**.

I magic-markered TENNIS across the front. I didn't want someone to put coffee in my prized souvenir. Any morals to this story? None that I can figure. Sir Bruce you schmuck . . . (Was Director Lynn his aunt?)

This 'book' may be my vengeance at last.

(Let's hope the editor of this book isn't a fan of Sir-Bruce)

I'm pretty sure Sir-Bruce doesn't even suspect any of this happened.

Years later someone told me he was a **Minister,** or a Clergyman, No-way! Ok, maybe a rector. . . . You know it kind of fits doesn't it.

Bless me father for I have sinned . . .

Father Bruce has the piddily runner-up glass cup in this
fantasy dream of mine.

My First Tennis Trophy

And first time meeting Frankie

I didn't really know Frankie.

As far as I was concerned, Frankie was a loud mouth. At this time, I was a very *serious* tennis player and losing meant I personally was a loser. Not a good tennis player but *serious* (before lessons and USTA). I searched out local tennis leagues to test myself against the outside world. Frankie was already a fixture in this new world.

He didn't look like an athlete, but he could play tennis.

Frankie was the voice of all the tennis players from the '*Hole*'. A tennis court tucked away in a small valley behind the stores in the quaint town of Wrentham Mass. A technically beautiful setting of grassy-sloped grounds, wide granite stairways accented by fancy wrought iron handrails. Rare old sycamore trees spread out for shade enticing you to enter. Walkways and benches litter the area with the tennis court as the main focal point of the park. Antique chain link fencing only on the ends, leaving the side's open. Stunning to look at but a nuisance chasing errant balls. I myself played these courts several times over the years, but not for the last few, due to deterioration and missing and fallen nets.

Frankie brought his own net each Sunday morning from 7 am to 1 pm.

The other net held together each week by tape, plastic twist ties and band-aids only lasting the few hours of play. This was craftily worked out to assure them a reserved court each week. Frankie's crew played together in some form or another every Sunday morning for the past 20 years.

Frankie was funny, unless it was you that was the butt of his jokes, and the jokes would fly from the sidelines especially while you were playing one of his clan. Alcohol added a little zest to the situation. I recall yelling from the court at Frankie to, "Shut up and have another beer!" He was sitting on his cooler at the time being a little extra rowdy, with a group of buddies. Not a friendly gesture on my part, but I wasn't making friends, I was in battle-mode and playing for my honor.

The fall tournament that ended the summer tennis season, was my first encounter with Frankie. We both lost in the first round, and that put us in the consolation Tournament. A separate tournament for the losers, of the first and second rounds. This is set up to justify paying 20 bucks to enter . . . No one wants to pay 20 bucks for one game. For the rest of the weekend I battled long and hard to be the best of the worst, the king of the losers (sort of). It all came down to me and Frankie.

This was my first year of tournament play. It was exciting and scary, with your game scores being displayed on the large score board for all to see, along with playing in front of a fairly large crowd of peers. Waiting for your name to be called matching you up with your next opponent. (Not my favorite part.)

Me versus Franklin, in the finals for the championship of the losers bracket, but wait, Frank had Red Sox tickets and had to leave early, so the bosses called a meeting and reschedule him to play the following night.????? What? That was his first default, then came a rainout and other excuses. Was he afraid to play me? I wasn't kind or friendly towards him; I was a bit sharp and even rude to him as he poked fun of me to get a few cheap laughs. He backed out of the next few dates they set up to accommodate him. He really didn't care about this consolation thing, it wasn't worth his effort so he finally backed out and the lucky loser, [What?] was brought back, and the finals commenced. "Just give me the trophy already, Frank defaulted*!!!!" Lucky loser* my Butt.

Yup, the guy who lost to Frankie, Steve Nespolo. So that meant he had already lost twice before being brought back to play for the coveted consolation plaque. Did you ever hear of such a thing? No!

Maybe he was just asked to play so I could have my court time. (I was naïve.)

The game didn't count I had already won !!!!!! Still it was promoted as Championship game.

This was big for me my first final in the tennis world. So I invited my Grandmother and Mother to watch. They had never seen live tennis and didn't know the rules. Especially the long, long warm up.

Technically, I thought I had won by default. That was my first mistake. I took the whole final thing lightly. In my mind I was already the winner . . . Not so. I won the first set but it was over an hour of pretty long slow physical demanding rallies. My opponent was playing moonball-backboard really well.

Mom and Granny had had enough, (the warm ups were enough for them) and bid ado. I was alone for the rest of the battle. In my mind, I was clearly the better player, but I was wearing down, I wasn't accustomed to the long physical rallies. He snuck out the second set. This was when I found out the trophy and my honor were really on the line. Wooo, and then I was informed the club and lights go out at 9 pm . . .

I was down a break 0-3 in the final deciding set, when on the changeover he told his girlfriend to wait around for the award ceremony. Ouchie-wa-wa.

20 minutes to right the ship. It had been a long day at work and a mentally wearing long game. I started to rush the net which was my best option; I had really good net skills. I never even gave a thought about being in shape. I played long matches before, but this was different I felt like I hit a wall. My legs were rubbery and I wasn't thinking straight. I don't remember the rest but I came out the victor just in time for the lights to go out. Collecting our gear and heading for the club entrance for the commemorative hand shake.

My first trophy (plaque).   **Consolation first place Winner!!**

My first trophy; I learned a lot from that tournament but it was only a smidgen of what was to come and Frankie was going to be a big part of my journey.

Steve (the replacement 'lucky double loser,') was also going to be part of my tennis life for years to come as he took over managing the summer league a few years later and becoming one of the better players in the league.

Mother and Granny never ventured to another match, but endured many homemade pizza nights listening to my tales of woe and elation.

Frankie called it the 'Booby prize'

The fat lady is about to sing!

The annoyed crowd started to slowly clap in unison
wanting the game to resume. Speeding up and
eventually turning into wild applause
when 'the Witch' finally sat down.
I'm Melting

'The Wicked Witch of the West Bleachers'

"TENNIS ISN'T ALWAYS JUST TENNIS"

My wife Laurie and I were getting pretty good at this tennis thing, for years we went to the Town Park and hit tennis balls. Inviting friends just for fun, but as we got better we sought out better competition.

This summer the local YMCA had advertised for group tennis lessons. Laurie cut out the newspaper ad and posted it for me. I got the hint . . .

Mrs. Davenport was the instructor, she ran drills very skillfully, and kept everyone busy and active. She made it fun. Laurie actually grew in her skill level fast taking the game seriously. We even practiced on the side doing similar drills, preparing for our next lesson. It became quite a challenge that I enjoyed.

Being complimented was addictive. One time Mrs. Davenport took me to a separate court and wanted to play me in singles **(testing me)**; she wanted to see how good I was. She kept telling me to play my best tennis, not to treat her like a woman. I still held back, and played defensively, just getting everything back. This of course was my game plan at the time. I remember her telling me I was easily a 4.0, she said it so 'matter-of-factly.' I was basically just a backboard, I could run down anything and junk ball it back. I had to find out what a 4.0 was. She had given me a USTA sheet that had player ratings on them with a brief description of each number.

2.0 = push serve / does not **know the rules** / can keep a rally going.
3.0 = good serve / **knows the rules,** good ground strokes, prone to unforced errors.
4.0 = great serve / **thinks they know the rules** / knows strategy / can hit winners.
5.0 = super serve / **knows the rules** / *doesn't need strategy*/ no one wants to play them.

It took Laurie and I ten years at least to become a '4.0'. I always wanted Mrs. D to know we did it. She was only there for that one season but made an impression on both of us inspiring us to go the next step.

We couldn't wait to join again the following year but she had moved on and the new instructor was just a kid.

The New Tennis Instructor; Mickey

Mickey didn't seem that young but it was actually his summer between high school and College . . . Mick had played tennis all his young life. Lot's of tennis. He had been seriously training since he was five years old with personal teaching Pros. The tennis club was his daycare and his after school babysitter. Tennis was a big part of his life.

He had been one of the best players on his championship high school team. I would have believed it except Mick didn't have the killer instinct. He was a friendly easy-going kind of guy. To him tennis was for fun.

The best player on his team was **Todd**, the best high school player in the state, maybe the nation, with the makings and prospects of going pro. He had enough killer instinct for the both of them, and left a dynasty of records and accomplishments in his wake.

Mick was the only player whom ever gave Todd any competition. They practiced together all through high school, causing a bit of tension between them. They were taught by the same coaches and played similar styles. Mick didn't have any ambitions of becoming a tennis pro, that was way too much work and he was smart, real smart. He wanted to be a lawyer.

Mickey was very laid-back and easy to talk to. He loved to see me coming to a lesson. He was usually bored, teaching kids and first-time adults all day; I pushed him to be more creative.

Mick soon became my next mission to smack down, (young blood) a new conquest. I challenged him and got his competitive juices flowing.

He was a very good instructor with very creative drills . . . All week he would go to several courts around the area teaching every day. As he said, "It was better than digging a ditch." We hit it off right away. He knew of all the local tennis happenings and tournaments; very in tune with the tennis community. He actually played singles with me a few times. Imagine teaching all day then playing with me. I was a good opponent for him; we were evenly matched at that moment. I challenged him but he enjoyed the fact that I listened to him and did what he taught. I became his pet project.

I quickly learned his weaknesses and soon had the upper-hand with him. Mainly I believe from certain things he taught me even as we played. Mick encouraged me to hit approach shots and take advantage of my good hand/eye coordination.

I became much more aggressive and charged the net volleying like a pro. This gave me a clear edge over most players and made me a better doubles player.

Funny enough we became close friends. I also met and played against his younger brother Adam, he was the current high school rising star. I believe he was only a Freshman. I of course dominated him, but what he didn't know was I had to work my butt off just to keep up and hope for errors (which I eventually got). At the end of that summer, Mick went off to college to become a professional sports contract-lawyer. WOW!

A few years into College Mick came home for a few weeks during his summer break. His now high school senior-sensation brother Adam, trashed-talked him into playing in the local Town Tennis Jamboree. Mick asked me to join him as his doubles partner. I was honored and excited to show him how I had improved and could only imagine how great he had become with a few years of college playing under his belt.

Mick set up a practice doubles match with his younger brother and partner, of course another high school sensation. They were undefeated their entire senior tennis season together. I couldn't wait to test them . . .

A lot of things got under Mick's belt, but none had anything to do with tennis balls or exercise. He didn't even want to look at a tennis ball, after his last few years of playing and teaching everyday.

Mick was heavier, out of shape, and hadn't hit a tennis ball in two plus years. His younger brother's team crushed us. Maybe this wasn't such a good idea. Mick was really not ready for this, he had

had a big breakfast, along with a bout of jet lag. (Yeah, that's what it was?) This was not the homecoming he was hoping for. Only two weeks before the big doubles tournament.

Tournament day finally arrived and we drew a couple of girls in the first round. Really, it was an open division. They were also high school phenoms. We struggled at first being gentlemen until they proved to be a formidable adversary. We came to our senses and over powered them.

Next up, a couple older gents (older than I was then.) We handled them easily. Getting through Saturday and into Sunday. We then had a good warm up match against a good father\son dual. They imploded and gave us clear sailing to our next opponents.

The current 'High School Doubles State Champs.'

Mick's brother Adam and his superstar partner; they came to the plate with confidence. They had dominated us in those practice sessions. This was the end of the road for us . . .

But wait, not so fast, Mickey seemed to have extra energy. He had been practicing and doing physical things the past couple weeks that kind of brought him back in game shape. He seemed vigorous and he knew his brother's weaknesses. (He wasn't going to lose to his baby brother) especially since the local newspaper was writing this story; "LOCAL COLLEGE BOY'S, '*HOME COMING*'—to take on baby brother's DREAM TEAM." They had predicted and hoped for this match up from the first night and advertising it with a two part special article Interview. A write up, about the brothers, stirring up excitement for the tournament. Not that they needed to. *I was just a side note*, touted as his former student.

The crowd was gathering early, (these guys had lots of friends), this was a pretty big event for the town, they loved the homegrown feel.

Well you've probably guessed (because I'm writing about it). That we won, and we did, not because we were suddenly hit by the gods of thunder, but because the kids were star-struck. At first it was them prancing around showing-off, having an easy time of it. However, as the crowds formed and the game got heated they started to fold. Big brother now had the upper hand. It didn't hurt our cause when they collided both going after a short lob, twisting an ankle and wrenching a wrist. Adding injury to their pride as well.

With Mom and Dad watching along with their tennis coaches, girl friends, newspaper reporters and friends cheering intensely, the stakes were higher than ever. They sulked, threw rackets, and became the John McEnroe twins. They stopped attacking, and played safe, which played to our strengths. They whined about every little thing, and while they were crying, we were steady. Winning the final two sets, yes the newspapers had something great to write about, *College Student's Successful—'Homecoming.'* This was more like it. With a front-page photo of the brothers shaking hands at the net.

Mickey was friends with everybody and because of his summer teaching camps; a lot of his students, young and old followed his return home. During the few weeks back he had visited the courts where he had taught and brought his racket hoping and getting a few hits, along with some needed exercise. He had worked himself back into form. His parents were so proud, and so grateful to me. Shaking my hand like I had just given them a million bucks. Maybe this is why I was invited to the big wedding?

The tournament wasn't over yet
Meanwhile, the Evil Empire in the opposite side of the draw was gaining momentum.

Mick's High school nemesis '**Todd**' (name changed to protect me).—Todd had won everything the last couple years, won the singles, doubles and mixed doubles. He would have been the town hero but he was an ass! The most arrogant, vain, self-centered, pompous idiot you'd ever meet. He would enjoy every minute beating even the weakest of players. Teasing and taunting, making them wished they never picked up a racket. He would even trash talk a crying baby while it was strolling by, embarrassing its mother, accusing them of distracting him.

He cheated—outright, (there was no honor in his vocabulary) every chance he got he would play dirty. He would cuss and swear, even force his opponents to change their calls. He was the guy you didn't want to play.—He didn't have to do this stuff because he was by far the best player around, but there was no college or pro contract in his future. He was a bitter kid that got away with it.

No real future at all . . . and his parents were worse, a real horror show! They taught and applauded his feistiness. To them it was gamesmanship, None of these yokels deserved to be on the same court with their superstar son.

Mom would stand at the end of the court outside the fence and threaten the other team, calling them cheats and liars. I couldn't make this up. Players would complain to the directors. They did nothing. Probably fearing their own safety. I was warned that this was a known problem, an on-going farce.

A few more set up details.

This year the antichrist 'Todd,' was playing with his younger brother who had just graduated the year before. A family double-dose no less . . . The younger brother Mitchell, wasn't as talented but he was coming into his own with big serves and bigger ground strokes. Mitchell seemed to be embarrassed by his parent's outbursts and meddling, but could throw a pretty mean fit himself. Most of the time they won easily so the wild antics were saved for the bigger matches like this one.

There were several matches going on. All divisions were playing, but we got show-court honors. Front and center,—bleacher seats loaded to capacity. The ice cream truck and Lemonade carts were in full swing.

The Game plan:

We decide to pick on the *young one,* keep away from Todd and make him sorry he was playing with his younger sibling. I was voted to be the **mean one**. Mickey had a reputation to uphold and this was right up my alley 'ACTING 101.' I didn't know anyone in the crowd. Maybe I shouldn't have given my real name at the sign up. We had told Mick's parents of our tactics so they wouldn't hate me. I started out early telling them what side of the court they could warm up on. I was much older than these guys, much bigger with a gruffly half-started beard. I tried to look as mean as possible, threatening with the impression of exploding. That was my job . . .

'Tennis isn't always about tennis.' We had nothing to lose, and this was the first time they had seen me.

It seemed to be working. I dictated everything. Loud and forceful taking them off stride at first.

Mick followed up apologizing for my rudeness. We took an early lead, which was a cue for Todd's parents to step up and move closer to the court. Mick hit a hard ball that they scooped up and fed to me standing at the net, so soft and slow. I over exaggerated a huge swing and plowed it into the younger kid's midsection, he doubled over as the crowd went silent, these were not well-liked people but this was vicious.

The first voice coming out of the silence was their mother calling me a brute. The crowd still quiet—I barked at her, "*Mind your own business—he shouldn't be on the court if he was a sissy boy who needed his mother's dress to hide behind.*" . . . Diabolical! I liked this role, I was good at it. She started a come back but I bellowed, "QUIET PLEASE!!" . . . Dead silence . . . I caught them off guard; nobody dared to put them in their place before, with the fear of retaliation.

Play continued fairly even-flow, no real incidence, the usual bitchin' and moaning but fair, as we *won* the first set. The ante was now raised. They had not lost before. They weren't supposed to lose. Mom and Dad started questioning our calls from the fence.

At one point I stepped out of character forgetting for a moment to be roguishly bad-mannered, changing one call that was close and gave it to them, but I was not supposed to be the nice guy. Anything remotely close on their side was a quick out call, they took every advantage possible. This time they took the lead, as Mick had a hard time finding the service box. They started to get energy from that break of serve. I tried to get meaner but missing a few easy shots put me in my place.

They won the second set with that one break. Ending the set, by smashing an overhead from a short lob off my forehead. Throwing my cap into the air. Standing at the net I never expected him to hit it toward me. There was an open court for him to push it into. It was a total surprise.

That was a nasty wake-up call. (I'm sure I deserved it.) Embarrassed and one-upped I got fired up.

This was the final set. This was war and I was back at attention.

They took a long bathroom break and left me stewing . . .

Turning my cap backwards, I started the final set serving with a vengeance. Neck and neck the game went. There were no close calls argued for the start of the deciding set. The boys ask their mom to back off and sit in the stands. Oddly enough they grew a pair of knackers/goolies /gonads /rocks /nuts. This became a game of honor . . .

A first for them.

I think they enjoyed being the good guys. They stepped up their game, but we had an answer to everything they threw at us.

Their Mom got anxious just sitting, she had a reason for being so vocal, so impromptu. They weren't wealthy in fact, poor was an understatement but they had their boy's and tennis was the only thing they did good, and she reveled in it. This was her time to shine.

This was the first time the brothers played together, the older one never had the time for the weight of a sibling holding him back, but this year Todd's partner backed out last minute with an injury. Mother seized the opportunity and forced the pairing of both children. A lot was riding on this tournament for them.

She wanted,—needed—an advantage for the boys. The score was too close and nearing the end. There was too much at stake to just sit and watch as the game went on.

There was plenty of great shot making and rallies, wooing the crowd. Everyone held serve, right up to the tiebreaker. Yes, a tiebreaker for the chance to advance to the semi-finals. First team to get seven little points wins.

This game meant everything to the—'antichrist'—family. To Mick it just meant a fun time back from college and a time to re-unite with old high school buddies. He had proven he could still play and was happy with how far we had gotten, in fact if we made it further it would have interfered with Mick's summer plans of touring New Hampshire and Cape Cod with his soon to be bride, before returning to college. This was just a family reunion for him nothing more.

He actually told me he did not want to win. (What?) He had never expected to go past the weekend.

Talk about taking the pressure off. That shocker made me a little punch drunk. A first class sucker-punch to the gut knocking the wind out of me. I was at odds but figured I would let the game take us wherever. I was not tanking this game.

I suggested we walk; just get in a shouting match with the wicked witch, pick up our stuff and walk off . . . The newspaper would have a field day with that. He didn't buy that grand exit. Alright, fake an injury.—No!—You don't have the heart to knock them out of the tourney. This is unheard of; I can't even fathom this situation. He knew them well and felt sorry for them. Mick has everything; they only had this one week in the tennis spotlight. I can respect Mick's thinking now, but at the time it didn't make sense.

Mick threw in a double fault to start the tiebreaker, (already a mini 'break' behind). I think he did it on purpose. I was dizzy with confusion . . . Next, the degenerate youngster threw in two aces. We were trailing 0-3 already.

It was up to me. I was hyper—steadying myself to serve. I reeled back and just let it fly, 100 mph down the middle, but it lifted and landed near the back fence. Wow! Was that off. ("Who cares?" I debated in a mental daze). They made me wait while they cleared the court as the ball rebounded off the fence. Instead of a safe second serve I hauled off on another bomb with reckless abandon, a clear ace up the middle, the crowd and the brothers were stunned as well as I was. Mom standing at the fence tells her boys to call it long. *"IT WAS LONG,"* she shouted, *"That's a double fault."* They started to call it out, well 'after the fact.' I didn't let them steal it. I just said, thank you for the returned ball and headed for my next serve.

I called out the score loud enough for all to hear. "Our point **1** serving 3". I had seen them bully points away from other teams, I wanted that point and I kept it . . .

Momma called me a cheat saying her boy's called it a double fault. I stopped play (the crowd went silent) as I walked over to her at the fence and whispered to her, gritting my teeth in my best Clint Eastwood. *"Lady make my day"* *"Go and SIT DOWN!"* I turned my back on her, picked up a water bottle and took a big swig. I didn't hear a sound as the other courts had finished and all eyes were on us. I wasn't going to continue with her at the fence. I stalled as the younger of the boys pleaded for her to let them play.

The crowd (mostly my partner's friends) slowly started to clap in unison, getting louder as more joined in . . . Embarrassed she waddled to the stands with her tail between her legs. She threatened, *"You'll be sorry,"* I muttered to myself, *"I already am."*

The unison clapping grew into cheers as I walked back and announce the score 1 serving 3. No arguments.

Yes, the adrenalin was like lightning as I hurled a monster serve right at the super-dude. On the bounce, it curved right into him and shot backwards ricocheting off his racket clearing the back fence like a rocket. Even I had no idea where it was going as I let it fly. We were only one point down now 2-3.

Fearing the worst, for the next two points I did everything I could to keep Mick out of the play as I took over the court. We each won a point, they were up 4-3 with my partner Mickey serving.

I walked over to him, handed him the ball, and had a chat; I seemed to convince him that **they** were going to win no matter how hard he tried. We couldn't win so come on and play hard. Mick got both of his service points and gave us the lead 5 to their 4.

Two points from victory. They served into a great rally of shots ending in a barrage of heavy volleys until they slipped up and tried to volley lob it over my head. I jumped and whipped an overhead right at the youngster. He couldn't get out of the way to let it go out of bounds, instead it hit him hard in the neck.

Mom couldn't stand this, "*%#!*^," she bellowed, over the roar of the crowd. One point from victory and she was lit on fire. She knew her boys where out, they had quit at this point totally giving up, and it was up to her to stop the game and change their luck.

Of course, I didn't want to delay the game with a chance to win on the next shot. So I bit my tongue and played through it, (bad idea) as they tied us and easily went on to win. Very anticlimactic with a polite applause to welcome us off the courts.

We lost but we were the real heroes that day.

I was fighting three players on the court and their Mom. All was right in wrongville as they say. Everybody was happy . . . Except me.

Luckily, I wasn't portrayed as a bully in the newspapers; in fact, I was touted for having the gonads, the moxie to stand up to the wicked witch of the west.

Mick really didn't want to win, never expected to win, as it was, we would have defaulted the next match because he wasn't altering his plans that week. He sabotaged me, but we still remain friends. I held a small grudge for about a week, as you can see. Other than his wedding and his Christmas cards, I never saw him again. I know he is doing sports lawyer stuff and he has two pug dogs and two cute kids, placed strategically on each card. Very little words except to say, "Hi, how are you—remember when?" "Ya, I remember !"

We didn't win that day, in fact, the knucklehead-brothers went on to lose in the next round to a team Todd had always beaten in the past. I heard Mom stayed home, she had been written up in that nights Daily Newspaper with a photo and all. Not very complimentary with her screaming and pointing her finger.—Giving her all the credit for the win. Talk about gonads.

I had heard she calmed down after that, but that was what she lived for. That was her 15 minutes of fame.

I don't know if the boys stopped playing or she had health problems. I had heard different rumors but never had the pleasure of her company since. The tournament got bigger and better as the years went by. I missed the next few years but always checked the articles and hype in the newspaper. Wishing I had been apart of it every year.

 *Disclaimer, this happened approximately 10 years ago. As time goes by, I become preponderantly more the hero; it's funny how the brain works. I don't condone head-games and I never stole a point that was not mine. Tennis is a game of 'Honor,' but sometimes you have to fight for your rights.

 This is my true memory of the event, but again I didn't do research, nor do I want to. I am sure all involved had different versions, if they remembered it at all. To them this wasn't a day of heroes and villains. It was just a tennis game. To me, it was life in a nutshell, a learning experience that stayed with me.

 The MORAL????

'Tennis isn't always just Tennis'

Is there a Doctor in the house?

"Dr. Hanky"

'The Ringer'

The Doctor only **Rings** twice

Take two aspirins and call me in the morning.

Being a late-in-life tennis aficionado, there are a few moments that molded and pushed my desire to improve, and justify all the work I was putting into the game. I wasn't even a member of a club yet, but I had played there a few times as a guest. My wife and I would sub-in on an occasional Sunday night if they needed extra players. I felt I was a good player, but I had no way, to measure how good I was. This meeting took place, well before I'd heard of the USTA rating system.

The coordinator at the club got in touch with me; it seems there was a guy who played late every Thursday night. He needed an opponent. He had paid in advance for a block of court time throughout the entire winter.

What did I get myself into? What if I couldn't compete with him? A swarm of doubts whirled through my head as I pulled into the club parking lot. I introduced myself to him; he forced out a quick hello, turning away to continue his conversation with his injured buddy who came to watch the beat down.

I stood alone waiting for the starting bell to ring. We walked out to the court in silence, as we pulled out our rackets he spouted, "You have to address me as Doctor, not just Hank." "Sure, and you can call me—ah, ah, ah,—Mike." I had several comebacks, but none fit the occasion. There was no joking today, this was serious business.

We had two full hours to play, and I was excited to be on a court during the winter. The warm-up went on forever, mostly ground strokes, if I hit the ball even a few feet to the side he wouldn't chase

43

it, instead he would just snarl and scrunch up his face. All the while hitting to me with an astonishing pace. No volleys or overhead warm-up for Hank; he pretty much stayed right on the baseline.

I couldn't wait to get started. I had been informed that I should be good to him if I wanted to play the rest of the month for zilch. I was ok with that.

We finally started to play a set; He served first and right off begun serving really fast. My guess was well over a hundred mph, straight up the middle every time, (very imposing.)

I could barely see it, but what I could see seemed to be long by only an inch or so (every time.) Trying to be accommodating, I played them all instead of calling a fault. I just leaned toward the middle, stuck out my racket and floated them back deep. No worries there, he never ventured in from the baseline. I charged the net once, (probably not the most hospitable thing to do), volleying a text-book drop shot. He didn't even attempt to run it down? He just snarled. I felt like I did something illegal, unethical. So I resolved to stay back at my baseline, to be friendly, returning everything he launched at me, deep and loopy. He continued blasting ground stroke after ground stroke, always aiming towards the same general area, my backhand corner.

He had an awesome inside-out forehand. I learned quickly I better head there before he even hit it. He just stood at the baseline and waited for me to miss, but I didn't miss. Hank profusely sweated, heading for the towel after every point, shaking his head in disgust. He psyched himself out. I never even hit my big topspin screamer. When I served I just threw in some loopy spinners (nothing fancy) just to start the point. Being friendly and all.

The set ended (6-2) in my favor. In my opinion it was closer than the score suggested. I was working hard, but evidently not as hard as the "Doc." It took about fifty minutes of our two-hour court time (including the long endless warm-up). Hank came to the net; I thought to switch sides, but instead he whimpered, "I don't want to play anymore, let's just practice our strokes" . . . Huh?

"You're too good you're a *Ringer*" and "I don't want to work that hard for a point." Sarcastically I pleaded with him, "Well, Doc, I thought it was a great set. A battle worthy of Kings . . . It's got to be worth another go, come on let's try one more set." He pauses, towels off his sweaty face, leans over and grabs his knees, takes a deep breath and reluctantly agrees. I had a feeling my free court time was fading fast. I decided to ease up even more.

I can't miss on purpose, but I could hit all the balls closer to him, so he doesn't tire. Let the chips fall where they may. Evidently they fell a little too far from the tree, and after a few games into this set, he again quits and suggests we just hit and play out a few points. *Oh yeah that will be fun?*

Knowing that I blew it this time, I figure I would just make the best of it, but to my chagrin he soon packed it in. "Hey, We still have an hour of free court time left," I grumbled to myself as I slowly packed away my racquets, looking around for a player to use up the final hour of court time. The place was a ghost town that late on a Thursday night.

Hang-dogging my way off the court Hank started accusing me, "You're too quick and too good, you're a *ringer!*" He soberly swore snorting, "The club set me up!" . . .

Wow, nobody ever called me "too good" before. This was confusing because he wanted a good opponent, a top-notch athlete.

I followed him off the court and slumped into the closest chair, disgusted, waiting for some feedback from him. He ignored me, so I just went home immediately phoning the coordinator to apologize for letting her down.

On the contrary, she actually worked with Hank at the Hospital, and he constantly bragged of his tennis prowess. She hated his arrogance and was extremely happy to hear of his crushing defeat. He, of course, left her alone from then on. Could I really be this good?

Wouldn't you know about two weeks later; on a Thursday night, I received a phone call from Doctor Hankie, asking if I wanted to play a couple of hours? It seems, he wanted to redeem himself, and give it another go, yeah right! I'll be there, oh—if I'm a little late, go ahead and start without me. Sorry Doc, the way you give up so fast, I hope you don't work in the emergency room. By the way Doc, "*What hospital do you work at?*" I'm staying as far away as possible.

As you suspected, it didn't end there.

Yes, another big tournament. Flash forward a *couple of years* down the road, and a bit more experience under my belt.

Every year for at the past hundred years or so, this industrial borough sponsored a tennis tournament to benefit the high schools tennis program, and court repairs. However, the kicker is . . . It's closed-off to the outside world, you must live in town to enter. This, they feel, keeps the **ringers** away and let's the locals shine and there are no shortages of local talent in this town.

It's big! An entire week dedicated for just doubles. The best part is the Daily Chronicle newspaper takes an extensive interest, advertising and writing articles complete with photos and personal interviews. Every night, front-page news for its large-scale multi-town following. Spectators flocking the grounds in the hundreds. A food vendor's haven with a carnival atmosphere. This is highly publicized so it became commercially sponsored with Championship rings, as trophies, valued in the thousand-dollar range to go to the winner. Proudly displayed for all to see. (Being a big jewelry town, this is not as odd as it sounds, they contract the Superbowl rings, NBA championship rings, World Series rings, etc.)

However, there is a loophole in the entree qualifications; if you worked and paid taxes to the town you could enter, or a resident of the town could bring an outsider as his partner. Lucky for me, My brother was working in this town in the jewelry business. I was no longer merely a spectator.

We entered the 40 plus senior division, but were mysteriously put into the Main Draw. (We found out later the old timers didn't want new-bees disrupting their long-time feuds). My brother and I were ok with that, we just wanted a weekend of play, never expecting to go much further. Hey, we joked, now we had a chance at the coveted Ring Trophy that was only given out to the sharp shooters of the 'Main Draw'.

Having set the table . . .

The start of the games landed on the 4th of July weekend the hottest day you could imagine with crowds of people roaming the grounds. It was mass confusion getting players to the right courts on a tight schedule. This first weekend weeds out the weaker teams fast with single elimination. If you win, you could play as many as three matches on Saturday and three on Sunday, with evening games played during the rest of the week.

The highest seeded teams don't even start until Monday, but most players showed up to scout the competition and enjoy the festivities.

Two things happened to set things in order:
The Hamburger vendor was passing out hundreds of **free**, complimentary, mini 'day-old' hot dogs, that spent the night in the back of his car, and second was the stressed 'Port-a-potty' spillage stench. A lethal combination, I will spare you the details. (Clean up—aisle five)

I counted at least five ambulances, at the site, for the players and spectators. My brother was hit hard, and was one of the first to go. Literally. (Sorry Richie.)

This was big cable news. You may have guessed one of the doctors flown in from the local Hospital (a few blocks away) to help out was,

"Dr. Hank." . . .

He recognized me immediately with a big smile and a hardy handshake, like we were long time buddies. He had me at a disadvantage, with all the commotion I didn't recognize him until the magic words. "It's me, Doctor Hank." I had only seen him that one night several years ago, and this time he wasn't wearing his tennis outfit.

At least half of the players were wiped out, not able to continue play. Having so much invested in the festivities, that were scheduled to end with a parade and colossal firework display, the organizers felt they had to continue the tournament. So they started to pair up the players who were left. Which ruled me out, I didn't have a sanctioned partner, I was an out-of-towner.

Dr. Hank being a tennis lover, followed the tournament over the past few years. He had always contemplated entering someday. Assessing the situation he came up with a great idea. He worked in

47

town, he had his gear back at the Hospital and his shift was ending as we spoke.

I reluctantly agreed to partner up with him, to face a much deleted array of adversaries.

"Think back."—Hank has a great serve and better forehand from the back of the court and I love being close to the net, especially with his approach shots. He made me look good, he put the pressure on, and I crushed any weak returns floating back across the net. It was a harmonious fit.

We were also very photogenic and an enormous hit, sparking interest for the daily newspaper and cable station. We became local heroes. The unlucky part was the best (top seeded) players got to rest and recuperate until Monday night. That was another reason the head office didn't mind pairing up the weaker players. In their mind, the real games didn't start until Monday night.

We both played better as a team than we ever could have imagined. Yes, we took advantage of a tough situation but that's what tennis is all about. Sometimes it's the sun, or the wind, and sometimes it's who is drawn for you to play first. Yes that's what we had, "the luck of the draw!"

We were the first outsiders ever to win, like a snowball rolling down the slopes squashing everyone in its path we got bigger and better with every spin.

Initially, they weren't going to award us the expensive **Ring Trophies**, because of the odd circumstances. They protested strongly at first. They actually told us that we couldn't have the expensive *rings* under these conditions and handed us generic plaques, from the local trophy shop. I wasn't surprised, but we did legitimately beat their grade-A players at the end of the week.

The Daily Newspaper was in our favor, with a great humanitarian story like ours. We made major headlines as they made us 'honorary-residents,' with a free pass to defend our title next year. The tournament directors had no choice but to award us the *rings*, and a key to the city. They didn't really give us any keys like I'd hoped. That was more of a nice gesture. It took more than a month to have the rings engraved and resized, but it was so worth the wait. They also appeared to be much smaller then I remembered.

We didn't defend the title that next year I believe Dr. Hank was transferred to another Hospital far away. I never saw nor heard from Dr. Hank again after that week. I do feel happier going to the emergency room these days, since I got to know Dr. Hank.

Believe it or not Doc's accusation of me being a *ringer* came true, as we both became Championship RINGownERS.

'ERIK ANDERSON'

Finding a teacher who won't smash all your dreams, dash all your hopes. Tear your teddy bear beliefs out of your hands and toss them over a cliff.
"Priceless"

Enter 'Erik Anderson'
On the court he is larger than life with a Booming voice, passionately pinballing around the court shouting tips, advice and strategies non-stop.

"My First Private Tennis Lesson"

With 'Erik the Barbarian'

I had been playing competitive tennis for just a handful of years at this point. A few local town leagues, tournaments, and lots of sandlot pick-up games.

My wife surprises me with a Xmas gift to beat all gifts, no not a super overpriced tennis racket, that was last year. A tennis membership at the local tennis club, a first for me. Clubs were taboo, too expensive and a den of man-stealing desperate housewives. A private lesson was something I had only dreamed of. I had just turned forty.

With a first-time membership came a few perks and free-bees, The Club's attendance had been dropping fast, and they needed fresh blood, so for a small fee you got everything: free court time, T—shirts, hats, balls, sweat bands, key chains, towels, etc. Best of all (a private lesson) with the Club tennis pro.

This sounds great! However, I started to hear from the grapevine that this "Pro" is no push over. He is known for running his students from the moment they hit the court. He was a no-nonsense self-proclaimed "**Blunt** man," a right in your face kind of guy. Don't waste his time . . . He will tell it like it is, no sugar coating with him. All Business!

I'm not just throwing sayings out, these were real comments given to me.

I arrived early and they pointed to the court where he was finishing up his previous lessons. They told me to get out there fast he was expecting me. That's odd, because I really needed a chance to stretch. I hurried out to the farthest court to join him. At the time I was fighting a basketball back sprain, and it took a while to loosen it up. I didn't even get the chance to talk to him before the lesson, to let him know I was just hoping to work on approach shots.

He was hitting me balls the moment I dropped my racket bag, no time to take a puff off my inhaler. We plowed right through the hundreds of loose balls on the court, dodging the last student who was still picking them up. Time was important!

He was loud, but I couldn't understand him (with a large empty building-echo and my poor hearing,) and I didn't understand the lingo. Open up your racket face. I was dumbfounded, what could that mean? I'm still not quite sure. Upon a miss he would ask, "Was your swing early or late?" Huh?

I wanted to impress him with my great skills, but he hit hard low balls at really tough angles, I had never had these kinds of shots hit at me in my games. I missed a lot, but he just kept ripping them harder. Slowly, I caught my breath and began to hit correct volleys, then adjusting my foot-work to keep my balance. I eventually hit a few with good pace and better angles. I don't think my actual lesson had even started yet, I was there pretty early.

He pushed me to the baseline and rifled deep ground strokes at me shouting, "Up the line" or "crosscourt." It took me a while to figure out what he meant. Calling out, "topspin" or "slice" with other commands as he ran me from side to side, adding a drop shot here and there. I wasn't known for my speed or my long distant running. I felt awkward; he was making a fool out of me. (I hated to miss even one shot,) never mind ten in a row.

He noticed I had a two-handed backhand and he would demand a one-handed backhand slice up the line. (What?) Ok . . . Then topspin lobs, slice lobs to the backhand corner. Huh? I would try it all, and within a few tries I would succeed in every one of his commands, (thinking I was letting him down taking so long to comply). I was totally exhausted and it was only 15 minutes into my hour long marathon. So many emotions.

He was a stern middle-aged man, stocky with a military hair cut and a loud drill Sergeant voice. No smiling, no joking, all business. Grabbing six balls at a time with one hand and firing them at rapid intervals. He was good at this, it appeared like he had done this *a few times before*.

He was testing me to see what I needed to work on, but the test went on forever. Each test getting harder, quickly moving on to the next test, bellowing tips, over and over until I obliged him. Opposite foot out in front on the volley, head still, stiff wrist, racket above the wrist, split step, small steps, explode into the ball, get to the ball quicker. So many tips . . . but they sunk in.

The hour came to a close, "thank god, I can't run another step." However he suggested we play a few real games for fun. He told me he had the baddest serve around and no one could touch it. The biggest, highest bouncing, kick serve, and he wanted to see how I returned it. He was right I had never seen anything like it, but I caught on fast and started to block them back deep into the court with increased frequency, racing to the net and volleying like I was the pro.

I was winning. It helped that I had just had an hour of drills, and saw his strokes over and over. I merely did what he had been telling me, it was simply another drill to me.

He made it harder, "We'll see if you have guts." Adding a new rule: *no second serves* and then another rule? You must serve and volley, (immediately run to the net) every time! "You've got to be kidding!" I was playing flawlessly by this time, in the zone, as I won that set. Was he still testing?

We then started another new set. I won that set at love, against the club pro! He was keeping the score.

He wanted to know, "*Do you come to the net this often all the time*?" I didn't know the rules had been lifted. "There is no way you just volleyed that ball, that skillfully off your shoe strings," he would say, while stroking his chin, squinting in awe, "but you did it over and over."

Then came my serve, I had pace and a wicked slice that bounced off the court into the side netting, with a pretty good up-the-middle shot to keep him honest. And my serves were on today (my back was loose by now) he couldn't touch them. (This was not normal for me.) Add to that a trick serve, *reverse slice wide* out to the backhand side, similar to a lefty serve, I called it the **corkscrew**. I was on fire, it had to be the adrenaline and all the drills together plus added focus.

He came up to the net and told me he knew I would have a good serve, by the way I hit my over heads. Then he quoted, "We are pretty equal in ability, (What?) but he would kick my ass with his mind." He lost that next set too.

The play was intense, and every time I thought I had won, and could finally relax he would start a new set, another hour had passed.

Finally—he'd had enough.

While picking up the practice balls scattered over the court together, he asked questions like, "How old are you? (That old!) How long have you been playing? Never had lessons before? Ever hear of USTA?" Asking me if I would be interested to play on his club team? I had no idea what that meant at the time. "Who are you losing to? I have to meet these people." Throwing compliments after compliment at me. I was confused, but euphoric. This is a true story.

I thought he was the meanest, baddest Pro-trainer in New England?

What did he mean, he couldn't believe how good I volleyed? He had just hit me thousands of practice shots, how could I miss? I was a little embarrassed as the compliments went on . . . I had gone ahead into the player's lounge where Bob at the front desk asked how I did. I was a bit dazed and exhausted as the club pro came off the court and continued the glorious compliments in front of everyone. Stating stuff like: there was nothing more he could teach me, I was at the top of my game and they had better snatch me up for the club finals etc.

I sat stunned. This was a dream everyone has to have. Taking lessons for anything: (Guitar, math, painting, knitting, writing) and impressing the teacher, to be showered with compliments in front of your peers. Am I dreaming? Sometimes truth is so much crazier than fiction. There had to be a catch, but I had already signed for a membership. If I hadn't been warned, by friends, about his being 'all business', this wouldn't have meant so much.

How could anyone compete with that day, I didn't want to ever let him down, or show him it was a fluke. I never wanted that feeling to be taken away from me. How could I tell my friends what happened. I sat in my car afterward and just bawled, the tears flowed uncontrollably. As corny as it sounds the whole drive home, I would throw my fist into the air and scream with delight woooooo! Right now, I can feel the emotion of that moment, my eyes are welling up as I type.

He did tell me to lose the trick **corkscrew** serve,—yeah, like that was going to happen.

I couldn't wait to get a pad of paper and write down all the tips and compliments he threw my way, about seven pages full. That was ten years ago. I just dug those papers out.

Was I that good? No . . . but I felt that good—that day! ("I'm on top of the world!")

The feeling carried over into my games for weeks. Over the next few years I played at the club, and joined the USTA, and learned all the tennis terms and rules, but stayed away from private lessons. Mostly because of cost and time, I used all my spare time and cash to play tennis.

About five years later I actually did see him again. Group lessons with several other guys, gearing up to go to the New England Sectionals. I went breathless as I drove up to the practice courts and saw him with my teammates. He didn't seem to recognize me, I had much shorter hair and a beard, ok, maybe a few pounds heavier.

I just jumped in line and braced myself for a whirlwind of drills. There were no compliments that day or the next several weeks for anyone. This was all business and he was in his glory, ten guys idolizing his every word. I made sure I was the first one there and the last to leave, I didn't want to miss a single tip, or quote.

To show our appreciation for his help the team paid his way to join us in Arizona for the Nationals. It was great that he could accompany us.

During the final night team dinner in Arizona. He got up and made a toast to the entire group stating that I was the team (MVP) of the Nationals that year. It was a great moment for me, in front of all my teammates with my wife by my side.

I will never forget seeing the smile on his face the whole time we were playing, and you could literally hear his voice, over the crowds, reminding you to split step, and chip and charge, etc.

He had commented several times that we (as a group) were the most exciting to coach over his lifetime of teaching, because we wanted so badly to do well. We soaked up everything he had to give, and made him proud to be a coach. He couldn't wait for Saturday mornings to put us through hell. I think we rejuvenated him as well. We drilled from 8 am sometimes to 3 pm. I doubt the $10 bucks each, (paid for that much time). Of course he jumped in and played with us as well. He always seemed to pick me as his partner, and I was in my glory.

He's a person I will never forget. I often wondered if he knew I was that guy who took that one free lesson from him, years before. Did he really think I was that good? I'll bet he never knew how much that day meant to me. That will last me a lifetime. I didn't need the old notes I had written, to remember this, but they did help to justify that it wasn't a dream to me. I have so much respect for this man, and his knowledge and dedication to the game I love.

His name is **Erik Anderson** based out of Cumberland, Rhode Island. Thanks Erik, for another great moment in my tennis life.

Erik had suffered a heart ailment after our trip to Arizona and was laid up for quite some time. I sent him a get well card thanking him for helping me get to the Nationals, and I added thanks for the great personal lesson years before—adding how much he had helped me, praising his teaching skills.

I saw him briefly again that next Xmas as he ran a holiday tournament at the club. He called me over to the side thanked me for the get well card and asked me what I meant about the private lesson. I was caught off-guard, and just said I would have to explain it at another time. I didn't get to talk to him about it. I had heard he moved to Florida to teach year-round outside.

Maybe I will send him this story. It is always a great feeling to know you did a phenomenal job helping out a student, even though it was just a few lessons, it was, as if I had him with me for years. I still remember the slightest details as I reach back to that day imitating him as I am teaching friends the game.

It's funny; he would often refer to his first coach to make a point, as I refer to him.

I was lucky enough to get to know him better. I respect him so much, which makes his praise mean so much more to me. I couldn't wait to get his address and send this draft to him, just to give him back some of the happiness he gave me.

This morning, (eight years later) I was playing tennis with my wife. We had just lost a tough match and were playing an extra set, for fun . . . I had noticed a truck outside the fence, I figured someone was waiting for an opponent.

As we finished our game . . . Erik got out of the truck and came over to me to shake my hand. He was just driving by and recognized me. He had waited nearly an hour to say hi. Of course I was overwhelmed, that he cared that much, He made me feel so special, as he told the others he hadn't seen me since Arizona and the Nationals, "How long ago was that?" he asked. I knew the date but held my tongue. He pointed out that I was the MVP and only made 5 errors the entire week of the Nationals. I swear—he was still complimenting me as we walked out to the cars . . .

The woman who was playing with us was a very high-ranking player trying to get a word in edgewise, removing her sunglasses she asks "Do you remember me?" He said "yes" mentioned her name turned and continued our conversation, he was there to see me.

I didn't let him down; I never had to worry he would think that day was a fluke. It was a good day for him as well. He wasn't trying to beat me, he was testing me.

Ok maybe he compliments many players, not just me . . . But he does it in a way that makes you want to play the game and do good for the coach. He made everyone feel they were the most important person to him.

I came down off my cloud long enough to ask him for his mailing address . . .

Thanks "Coach"

THIS WAS THE RETURN LETTER FROM ERIK

Michael,

Well, Well, Well! . . . Hope this letter finds you happy and healthy. I have never been one for accolades. I do my job well and enjoyed all 42 years of it, and I still enjoy working teams into the districts and sectionals. I mentioned to my wife that I ran into you last summer and she remembered the dinner speech in Tucson, as I cast my vote for MVP of the team.

When I read this rough draft I said to Brenda it reads like a book, not like an article. My passion has finally paid off in the highest compliment you can give. I am impressed with your writing style. A great writer can paint so many pictures in your mind and you have mastered this art. I would love to add this to my memoirs, if I ever find time to write them.

In my years of teaching I have had many pros under my direction (most have not been good.) The one thing that is most important in teaching anything is passion. My energy level was above average because the student taking a lesson at four pm paid just as much as the student that took one at nine am.

Believe it or not humility plays a strong role in teaching. Always make the student feel that they are better in the pros eyes, but never under false pretenses. I still teach but won't do any high level juniors because of my age even though I feel great. My heart issues (quad bypass) were genetic and the doctor gave me a 20 year warranty.

Keep me posted on the progress of this book. I told my daughter about this and she wants to know when it is going to be published. Any future thoughts you might need don't hesitate to quiz me, I will see you this summer and we will talk.

Kind regards,
Erik 'the Barbarian' Anderson.

I CAN'T EXPRESS THE FEELINGS OF JOY READING THIS LETTER HAS BROUGHT ME.

MY own Kilimanjaro AdVEntuRE

'The Mile High Club'
"Do Bears Sit in the Woods"?
Bla—Bla—Bla

The elevation caused many problems but the weather was superb. I had prepped for more than a month doing cardio, jumping rope, and sit-up crunches by the hundreds, but nothing could prepare my lungs for what was about to happen.

My tennis team made it to the Nationals. A super team of, late bloomers most in our forty's. None of us had previously played USTA. Winning a trip to Arizona representing all of New England to take on America. An adventure I will never forget, especially at 4,000 feet above sea level in Tucson. Playing: New York, Maryland, the Caribbean and Hawaii, in a round robin. We succumbed to the talents of our opponents, but we were now free to explore the area the last full day of our **now** Vacation.

As a group, (my wife included) between matches we did some sightseeing, all the ritual Indian, and religious sites around Tucson. This traveling thing was a new and wondrous adventure for us. I am now, an official Tourist. I wanted to stay and watch the tennis finals, but was adamantly over ruled.

We had co-rented an SUV-vehicle with another couple, and they voted to leave Sunday morning at sunrise and head for the Grand Canyon. At first, I wasn't so enthusiastic about sitting in a car the entire last day of my trip and losing the final day of our prepaid (with no refund) hotel reservations. Now having to charter another hotel room in downtown Phoenix later that night for a full last-minute price. After I thought about it, then mulled it over a little more, I agreed whole-heartedly. That was a great idea! I hope it has a pool.

60

We had stopped for lunch in Sedona along the way buying t-shirts and souvenirs, enjoying the sights. Taking photos standing and waving in front of every possible mountain rock formation and tourist trap.

At lunch, we happened to notice another couple from our team dining as well, of course we joined them. They were heading for a wondrous hidden hiking trail in town, easily convincing our partners to change our plans to go with them. They had purchased this expensive secret treasure map weeks ago on-line. Our driving companions had already seen the Grand Canyon, and were easily swayed to join the hike right now and nix the Canyon jaunt that was still a couple hundred miles away. Which meant I no longer had any say in the matter? We had no choice, but it didn't really seem like such a bad an idea. We had loved hiking at home with the dogs. The more we thought about it, we began to favor the hike. I was a little miffed we weren't involved in the decision but soon enough came to grips with it.

We were officially a gang, a barbershop sextuplet, a mob, three teammates and their wives, with the opportunity to bond in the Great Outdoors. B.F.F. We're going for a walk-about.

I was beaten up from the grueling tennis matches, not so sure I wanted to scale a mountain, ford a river or sweat out a rain forest. I was dressed for eating and looking, in tourist fatigues not exactly suited for mountain climbing. Come on, how tough could it be? Who wants to see a Grandtastic hole in the ground anyway?

Hey! . . . We could walk around and kick up some dirt for a few hours, the landscape had been breathtaking en route. It could be fun if we just give it a chance. Maybe I shouldn't have eaten so many El Grande Buffalo burgers, (real Bison,) thinking I would be sitting, and relaxing the next few hours.

With a bit of effort we found the prized hidden entrance. We had the special secret trail marked out for us, saved for royalty and anyone who wanted to pay the big bucks. Being a late Sunday in October it was a surprise there weren't any hikers out today. *I hope* *there wasn't an accident or a **Bigfoot** sighting . . . The Rangers (men who sweep the paths for lost hikers before dark), had closed early and gone home. We begged . . . "Just let us walk around the bend." . . . "NO!" . . . They were closing and the gatekeeper was leaving.* We were never going to be this way again so we chipped in and offered a hundred bucks 'cash' extra, if she'd let us go in. No way, not without a guide as she nervously locked up before we could make a better offer and drove off. *Looks like its back to the original Grand Canyon deal.*

Of course, I have to whine about how much I was looking forward to the big mysterious super-hike, bla bla bla. But nooooo, only a lousy three hours before dark. I ranted and grouched from the comfort of the huge plush back seat. Now we wouldn't even have enough time to make the Grand Canyon before dusk. Wait a minute, the gate wasn't locked it was just latched shut. This could be the start of a bad 'B'-movie, or the beginning of a great adventure. We were like teenagers jumping out the bedroom window heading for a kegger with the excitement of going against authority. We were in charge! This was the balls, and we had the map. We're adults we don't need no stinkin' guide.

Bona fide Explorers!

The new plan;

Nightfall was in 3 hours. So we could walk as far as possible in one and a half hours then hustle back. EASY. Just stay on the charted path!

Cougars, Bobcats, Rattlesnakes, Tarantulas, and Grizzlies, no problem. It was total sunshine right now and HOT! "There hadn't been a Grizzly sighting in ten years," the map-holder reads aloud. **Sedona** was nearly 5,000 feet above sea level, (over a mile) my eardrums had already popped. By this time, I had three wads of gum in my mouth chewing like a madman. It had helped my ears on the plane. The air was so thin I was already wheezing with excitement exiting the car.

Back at the restaurant, there was talk of the Devils Bridge and a sinkhole called the Devils Kitchen, Soldiers Pass and the Grand Piano rock formation. I was excited, "let's go look at rocks." We grabbed our water supplies and started following the set trails with the easy to read secret-path-map. The huge sign at the entrance was a chilling reminder of possible dangers, 'YOU SHOULD NOT BE HERE AFTER DARK!' It is too dangerous climbing in the dark, and dusk is feeding time for Bears. Spelled out with large capital letters for all to see and TAKE HEED! ENTER at your own RISK! Not responsible for your safety. And in small letters it read "*if you have to poop, please bury it,*" eeeuw. I thought of all those bison burgers. All three of the port-o-potties at the entrance had been knocked over. From the looks and stench, I bet at least two days ago. I won't go into the ghastly details. My first guess would be young hooligans. I didn't notice the claw marks on the side until much later.

Checking out all the stunning sites took a while as we had to soak it all in and pose for photos. It was a bit of an exhausting heat that felt well over 100 degrees. I was already tired and drenched in sweat, so much for dry heat. It didn't help that while playing tennis the last few days I had sunburned my whole body.

The red rock cliffs were amazing. Stepping on strategically placed rocks to cross over brooks, then up and down a steep winding path. It was exhausting but well worth it. The red sandstone formations glowed a brilliant ruby scarlet in the late day sun. For a New Englander, this was impressive.

The odd looking twisted mesquite trees and the small pancake cactus set the scene of an old western cowboy movie or a cartoon with little roadrunner birds checking us out as they raced by "meep-meep." I looked around expecting Wile E. Coyote to be close by. At the end of the hour we had a group intervention—'turn back or go on.' The map told of some beautiful formations just ahead around the bend. We were all tired but decided to soldier on, so close to the big money shot.

At this point, my blisters were opened again, and the moleskin patches were pushed to the side. Just slogging along, following the butt in front of me, not noticing the scenery. I have to force myself to look around. I'm tired of the panoramic beauty, tired of being in awe, just tired. I was inventing new names for this particular trail, which I will keep to myself. A noise forces me to glance upward; I see a screaming pair of red-tailed hawks mating in midair. Oh my!

The time keeper proudly proclaims, *"We've reached the halfway point, an hour and a half."* We all debated about going a little further or turning back now. I voted to go on. What? I thought they meant, we were at a halfway point around the mountain, and if we kept going we would circle back to the entrance . . . The thin air must have cut off oxygen to my brain.

It was less than a mile to the big payoff of magnificent views like waterfalls and more rocks, etc . . . Another ten minutes to *more beauty?* Maybe I should have looked at this map.

Damn, I voted to go forth, not realizing we had to backtrack the whole route. I was dead tired now and limping. The trip back should be quicker if we don't stop for pictures, but that means no breathers. We all wanted to turn back, but no one wanted to admit it. They had talked it up as if it was the eighth wonder of the world, and made us give up the Grand Canyon. No quitters here.

Not to mention, my teammate Mike, (the one that dragged us here) had a much more severe knee sprain and was limping heavily. The terrain aggravated it, but he didn't want to be called a wimp. He had bragged about climbing Mt. Kilimanjaro just last summer, (in great heroic detail.) "The highest point in Africa, tropical rain forests, snow capped mountains," . . . "bla, bla, bla, "It took five grueling days, *You had to look down to see the clouds,"* "bla." I was envious.

Is that how I sound? Everybody's vacation adventures are great to them.

X marks the spot

Finally, we made it to the end, and it was well worth the energy. It was some kind of Devil's name like Satan's butt cheeks. What a great name, it really did look like a giant ass sticking out of the cliff as we watched the water trickle over it. It might not have been the eighth wonder, but it was somewhere in the top twenty.

Watching the clock, we knew we were a bit over the time schedule, but the sun was setting, and we had to witness it's breathtaking shades, tones and vividness of coloration for ourselves and try to get pictures.

A Five Alarm Autumn Sunset. Just thinking of it brings me back immediately to that moment in time.

This was so worth the effort. I finally had my own Kilimanjaro adventure to share.

BUT, not such a good idea. Suddenly, we had a chill of terror strike us because it was noticeably darker. Duh! Hence the term sunset. We rush out and back down the path with Mike (the mountain climber) limping up the rear . . . The other three were literally sprinting ahead with the fear of bears looming. It wasn't funny anymore. My wife and I stayed with the limping fellow, so we were slowed a bit. The others got out of sight as it became hard to make out the path racing back, the trail seemed to have many extra wrong options I hadn't noticed before. Did I mention the high altitude and the difficulty of breathing for an asthmatic, tired one at that? We yelled for them to wait up, but they went rushing far ahead. The streams were hard to navigate; the rocks were underwater, as the brook had risen. We just forded the river; wet feet were the least of our problems at the moment.

What was going on in my head? Slow down, Think! Climbing and hiking at these altitudes is a *mental* process, an exercise in concentration and will power. I panicked, we had at least an hour more to reach the safety of the car. I noticed certain thoughts sapping my energy. Which introspections worked best? *The ones that didn't have fear.* I must compose myself.

I was now cold and shivering, my t-shirt that was drenched in sweat is dried hard and itching. How about visualizing a nice warm swimming pool, palm trees, hot tubs and a big warm vibrating bed.

I glance at my sneaker and saw the sock drenched in red, a new blood blister burning, and stinging formed on my ankle . . . The ground is spongy under foot, I am light headed, and my inhaler has been overused as I gasp and wheeze. I stop for a moment bend over and grabbed my knees. I still can't catch my breath, not dangerous just uncomfortable. I try not to panic; realizing it's not going to get better we trudge on.

The thin air makes me feel like I am marching through water, in slow motion. When we came this way earlier I hadn't noticed the piles of god forsaken loose jagged stones, broken off by the many feet that came before us. Nothing looked familiar to me. My wife was guiding us back with the sixth sense of a true trail rider. Lewis and Clark would have been proud. Thank God someone paid attention.—Now may be time to start praying.

The darkness fell swiftly as we pulled our friend along. Hearing sounds in the trees and behind boulders . . . rattles . . . growls . . . small prey being attacked . . . wings fluttering.

A clatter of hooves warning us to hold still for a moment.

We tried to be quiet, but that was impossible. Heavy breathing, heavier footsteps and rustling brush, we were a prime target. *The weak straying from the herd.* There was something large up ahead lumbering oddly towards us. We jumped off the path and headed up to higher ground hoping to find a short cut. We were only halfway back, nothing seemed recognizable, we were lost and now we were dinner. The terrain was treacherous scaling the side of a cliff. Looking down we could see better because we were out from the trees, the rising full moon somewhat lit the way. I didn't have hiking boots just brand new tennis sneakers I had just purchased, now sopping wet, stained red from the clay and blood. Slipping and sliding over the loose rocks they'll be broken-in by the time I get back.

I had grabbed a branch for protection I was prepared to fight to the death (hopefully not mine). Mike grabbed onto the stick, and I pulled him along easier, quicker. Sacajawea couldn't help us out of this mess.

I started to fantasize as we trudged on.

Remembering a news flash driving here on the car radio. There's at least one body found every week in the Sonoma desert, usually too decomposed to be identified, I wondered how close we were to Sonoma, and how many do they find out here? I came up with a ingenious plan, (**a pipedream**) if we get stranded, we can eat the limper, and we could just say we lost him. I was getting hungry;

it had been a couple hours since I had last gorged myself. I could use an arm to bribe the bears to leave us alone. If we could lose the gimp we could make much better time. The thin air was giving me hallucinations. Mike was laboring, hinting for me to piggyback him. I was feeling a little randy; if we were alone I could consummate our marriage right here in the jungles of Africa (Me Tarzan). I was turning savage resorting to Neanderthal. I wanted to howl. The very next second I was fixing to pass out from the lack of oxygen to my brain. It was all so overwhelming I was fading fast, ready to give up. If I could just click my heels three times and transport home . . .

I believe it was National Geographic that had a program about facing a Grizzly in the wild. "Climb the nearest tree, "if there are no trees, DON'T RUN! DON'T look him in the eye.—Back away slowly. If he charges go limp, play dead. Does that mean he will give you hugs, and a playful wrestle? Easier said than done. He will only gnaw on your leg for a few minutes then get bored and wander off. That's some major Attention Deficit Disorder. I'm taking my chances and running, so I can enjoy my last six seconds on earth before a thousand pound behemoth sits on my head, and he will, sit on your head.

Black bears are the complete opposite, they climb. If you're up in a tree, you will just be fighting a bear in a tree. Yell at a black bear; throw a stick or rock, run at him waving your arms? You first!

There was a disclaimer—A Warning! If he's hungry enough, that may provoke him . . . Playing dead is not good with them, they will chew on you until your past caring. Well, that clears that up. Better yet, you only have to be the fastest runner in your group, or if you're the slowest you could pull a Tanya Harding. Oh, yes! All bears love candy bars especially Snickers.

I tapped out the last drops of water. My left ear tickled and felt muffled like it had liquid in it, that's a sure sign of dehydrating. That and being so thirsty I could drink from a mud puddle.

Experts warn without irony, to drink your water while you're still alive, as it won't help later.

I wondered how the others were doing. Did they make it back to the car? One false turn could be a nightmare, as we are finding out.

We were far off the beaten path when, Mike held us up for a moment to split his last candy bar with us. A Snickers! Oh Crap! Bears can smell that on your breath a mile away. This ought to even the odds of meeting Yogi and Booboo.

Scooting over a sizable boulder, we noticed streetlights in the distance if we could only make it over the ridge and down the incline. We did but there was a ten-foot high fence; I imagine to keep the wildlife off the highway. We had to climb the fence because the brush and topography was impassable in the dark. We traveled the last mile down the road and entered through the main gate, relieved to see the two women huddling in the car, anxiously awaiting our return.

Our other comrade Chuck found a feeble flashlight and a flare gun in the car and started after us calling out and shining the light hoping to guide us home. Someone told him to make noise, or whistle to warn the critters, so they wouldn't be caught off guard. He was whistling like nobodies business.

I went after him alone, leaving the limper and my wife in the car to warm up. My breathing and blood pressure were in better control now knowing I was safe.

Just around the first bend I met up with the him, of course I decide to play a childish prank as I tossed a small log over by him, he panicked and ran away from the cars into the woods. He would never have suspected it was me coming from the entrance side. The joke went too far as he shouted, "I have a loaded gun." It was the flare gun from his car; he tried to fire it, nervously fumbling, doing his best Don Knotts/Barney Fife impression. I called out, "Chuck, it's only me don't shoot." He roared back several expletives I wasn't even familiar with.

Thankfully it was not a flare gun, just a road flare. We lit it and walked back together holding it high above our heads.

A foul smelling bouquet in the air was a hint telltale. (I shouldn't have thrown that branch). I pushed out a manly sniff and proudly declared, "My bad," as we whistled our way back to the car. Reaching the safety of the car Chuck mentioned, about twenty minutes ago he thought he had finally heard us coming around the bend. When he rushed to meet us, something big and clumsy quickly bolted off the path and into the thick underbrush. "It took my breath away, it must have been a bear or something. It seemed to be more frightened of me."—Ohhhh man!—That was us!

We drove into Phoenix booked a room next to the airport and went to a late dinner, "I had to have a few grizzly bear sliders and some buffalo wings,"—not a good choice—but I was as hungry as a mountain lion. We all fantasized about getting tattoos to commemorate this week's adventure. My wife and I decide on a cactus holding a tennis racket. I'm game.

Wide-awake we snuck out of our room well past midnight, not wanting the adventure to end, and jumped in the massaging-jet hot-tub, enjoying the big harvest moon and the wide-angled starry sky. Taking pleasure in the mountains in the distance as they appeared to be flashing, with a dry heat lightening. Seizing the moment and savoring the cool pool water for a while, then back to the hot tub. Ahh this is the life, no lights just a full moon. The pool area was closed, but not for us, we were expert fence jumpers. Our traveling companions joined us. They didn't want it to end either as they turned the hot-tub jets up full blast.

We were home the next night to bone chilling Boston. Man was it cold from 110 degree sunshine to a cloudy 40, just ain't right. It took me two weeks to adjust, to the time and the cold and the depression of the big adventure ending.

Over the next week, I told my stories to anyone that would listen but all too soon I noticed they really didn't want to see more of my vacation photos. I know my romps in the wild are tame compared to Mowgli, the jungle boy or Laura Ingalls Wilder. All too soon, I notice their eyes glazing over into a glassy stare. I was fooling myself and sadly put it all on the back burner. I can still hear myself embellishing to friends, "*You had to look down to see the clouds,* bla, bla, and bla."

You can see we didn't travel much.

Over the next decade, my wife and I have had a yearning to go back. That is so odd . . . but it really is pulling us . . .

Three hours may not seem like much, but under the conditions, it seemed like a lifetime. The Boston marathon is run in three grueling hours, and they only have one heartbreak hill. You get the idea.

The Sedona Vortex is pulling us back like an inner body magnet.

We really feel it, yearn for it. Bla, bla, bla.

It's a bird it's a plane . . .

"It's *Super* Dave"

TRIPLE 0007
Soul Searcher
'Nitro' No mask—no cape . . . just a tennis racket and sneakers

Dave was the fastest person I have ever played tennis with and I've played with some fast people. Dave was nitrous-oxide faster than any of them. So *rocket* propelled that you had to repeatedly comment on his quickness because you were constantly being amazed. 'Turbo charged Nitroglycerine'

The local YMCA started a tennis league. It seems the new director of recreation was an avid player and he had a plan. Tennis in the USA was on the rise spiriting a major interest in the game. Tennis had become a macho swashbuckling sport with superstars like Andre Agassi and Pistol Pete Sampras leading the way.

About ten people signed up for the spring league. For some reason this brought together a group of local misfits, that had gotten the fever to check their skills and abilities against a new talent pool. These guys didn't know the all rules, hadn't taken lessons as kids, and didn't belong to any tennis clubs.

Like me, they had been playing with friends and now they wanted to expand their horizons. I was the best in my own small group of friends, and I needed to see just how good I was.

After the first weeks initiation the director lost interest and abandoned us. He handed out schedules and phone numbers leaving us on our own to figure out the rest. Wanting to play really bad I took charge. This was very encouraging to me along with the excitement of playing the unknown person. I met three of my best friends in this band of misfits including the aforementioned *Super* Dave.

Dave was an intense athlete, he immediately immersed himself in every aspect of the game. He dressed the part, the newest, hippest, hundred dollar Nike sneakers, sixty dollar tennis jersey and cap along with the official Andre Agassi tennis racquet. He was the best outfitted tennis player I had ever seen. This guy meant business.

Dave was as serious as you could get. He had signed up for every tournament on the east coast. I believe he had genuine dreams of going pro. The only problem was his advanced age [27]. Most pro tennis players retire around 30 if they make it that far. Possibly the only obstacle that could have gotten in his way, was his age.

Dave and I became hitting partners, he wanted to prepare for his tournaments and I was available. We eventually became good friends as he invited me to a couple of nearby tournaments, and even suggested we play doubles together. As teammates we fit together well. Dave was smart, he knew the game inside and out but his main strategy was intimidation. His battle plan was to; 'Take over the net.' I liked his enthusiasm, along with the excitement of competition, that made me feel young and energized. We both improved fast playing hours together, but as Dave improved so did I exponentially. So I was always a little better. This frustrated Dave, he wanted so badly to beat me. This gave him a mission.

David's antics wrote out like one of Freddy Prince Junior's romantic sports-comedies. To give you an example; Running to fetch a wide angled shot Dave jumped onto the chain-link fence, and hurled himself towards the ball. His heal wedged in the fence and there he hung upside down. It took three people to get him down. The very next play he dove, full stretch, on a tar surface to make a play. This was a routine *Super* Dave effort. The director of the tournament immediately called for an ambulance to have paramedics on stand-by. His quote to the EMT was "We have a bleeder."

He was so quick, he took over the net smashing anything near him, celebrating each smash with a touchdown dance, and a loud he-man Schwarzenegger squeeze-grunt. Especially beaming if he could bounce the ball over the fence into the parking lot. This caused opponents to become frustrated and hit at him, (he was hit a lot.) It became our running joke . . . if he wasn't hit; he wasn't doing his job.

I videoed a few of our doubles matches. This one sequences of clips we sent to Funny Home Videos: I hit a lob, but it was extremely short, I yelled for Dave to "watch out!" He decided to cause havoc as he ran up to the net directly across from the smasher, waving his racket and stomping his feet to distract him.—Dave became the smashee, (bulls eye direct hit in the crotch.) It made good TV as he rolled on the ground among cheers and jeers. He wasn't in the running for 'sportsman of the year.' The very next play I served a hard spinner into his back, I could see the ball stuck on his back spinning. He just laid draped over the net for the next few seconds in pain as the crowd gave him a standing ovation. We brought out the video this year at Christmas and had a good laugh. I actually made a sculpture of him hanging over the net to commemorate this moment.

The following year Dave and I joined a multi-town league just a few miles from me. As doubles partners it didn't take long before we improved enough to make the post-season playoffs. We were viable contenders at last. But, just when the 'getting-got-good,' Dave had a problem. I thought it was girl trouble, because he had started to bring his girlfriend who couldn't wait to get away from tennis and me. I didn't see much of him that year as he narrowly made it to the games on time and barely finished before he drove off into the sunset. The game became a bother to him but while he was playing he was truly in a better place enjoying every second. Any personal problems he might have had were far away while he concentrated on the tennis.

We normally played extra sets for fun, but now he would practically leave before the handshake. After a match that I had begged him to please play one more set, he confessed, "He was late for a special training session." I figured it was paintball. He was always heading to the airport for another quote; "professional paintball tournament." Paintball took him all over the world. Did they really have paintball in the Middle East?

The woman he brought to the matches was not his girlfriend, I found out later she was his training partner. The last day of the season they arrived at the tennis court in a fancy black car with peculiar license plates and military stickers on the heavily tinted back windows. There was something definitely taking over his life. Was it work, money problems, girlfriend, paintball or worst was he ill. I just wished he would let me know, maybe I could help him. Could he be involved in some special undercover secret agent project?

No side tennis tournaments these days; in fact he had no time for his Mom anymore. I was always so proud of the way he treated his Mom, to me, it showed a great quality in him. Not worried about being a mamma's boy or being embarrassed by his Mom, as often children were. They were best friends. She was a single mom and raised Dave by herself spoiling him the best she could and boy, *she could.* She did a great job with him. She thought of herself as an enabler. If she was an enabler, it was in a positive way. They were pals, and he included her in many of his activities to this point.

Dave had recently bought a home, Mom of course, came to live with him.

He had done well with his business ventures and was on his way to the good life, acquiring a luxury fishing boat, dog and cat, sporty pick-up truck and fancy new sports car along the way.

Something big was in the air. This is where details grew a little foggy, *I never asked for the facts, I don't really need to know them,* but from conversations, I made a few conjectures that I will pass on. David implied he was leaving maybe never to return. He gave me a few suggestions for a replacement as he quit the team. "Maybe someday we could play together once again," he sighed. I was not to ask him the details just to be a friend. His physical appearance grew worse each time I saw him even though he said he was training more than ever. Stress seemed to be taking its toll mentally as well.

This is when Dave asked me to take *care of* his Mother until he could get back on his feet. Oh yes, his cat and pitbull too . . . I took in his Mom and his cat; even his priceless baseball-card collection (over 50 trillion cards,) but I put a hold on the young energetic pooch. I had a Rottweiler already and they did not get along. Each vying for the attention of my wife.

*   *   *

There were a couple different scenarios about Super Dave's sabbatical; I'm sticking to this one. He is writing his own book if you're interested, but it will probably never see the light of day if the government gets wind of it. My other conjectures were poo-pooed by **The Powers That Be.** (TPTB)

Dave may have been recalled back into the special forces on a secret mission. So secret he couldn't mention it to anyone. I'd like to think it was possibly a mission to capture the Ayatollah Khomeini. At one vulnerable point he hinted of a casualty. Was it his partner? Whatever happened was going to leave a permanent mark. He may have been referring to losing himself or his soul. (His life force.)

My guess is . . . Dave was a Secret Agent, and his cover was playing paintball circling the globe with a team of covert all star recruits. Highly trained in warfare and weaponry—probably an unfair advantage in the paintball war games. (He is proudly planning to participate in this years Olympics.) Another mission perhaps?

Whatever this mission was, it affected him so deep he had to withdraw from the human race—maybe forever. Was he headed for the Himalayas the highest regions of the world or father north into Tibet, entering a Zen Buddhist monastery or maybe a Midwest Indian reservation to do some soul searching with the red tail hawks to recuperate? Dave was not heard from for years. Yes, if your speculating this to be too farfetched. It's possible I may have taken a little liberty with this. My artistic license is stretched to the breaking point. But just the same it all does fit perfectly.

I did ask Dave to verify this for the book, of course he was vague at best. Stating the old joke, "I could tell you, but I'd have to kill you."—

Say no more. He asked me to drop the subject as a friend. There was talk of him working for the 'Men in Black,' mostly in jest, but most jokes have some facts based in them. Also remember his Mother moved in with us and we had many long talks about David's surreptitious life traveling the world. 'TPTB'—have informed me to make this sound improbable if I want to add it to the story. All in all maybe he had a breakdown, the world as it is today can damage a person in a blink of an eye. So I leave it for you to decide. Wink-wink nudge-nudge.

During his sabbatical he turned off all communication with the outside world. Dropping off the edge of the world. We thought the worst.

Dave lost all his personal possessions because he no longer made payments. His new sports car was returned, his fishing boat went to a friend that was to take over payments and enjoy the boat, with the option of Dave taking it back at some point. His friend hadn't made a single payment as it was repossessed a year later. Now that's a friend. He gave the title to another close friend to sell his truck for him. The week he left his friend bought the truck himself for a dollar, and kept the dollar.

Dave had upped his mortgage to take out a huge loan, now the monthly payments were too much for his mom to stay there alone. So he came up with a plan. Mom came to my house and . . .

His Home was to be rented out for the duration using 'Chapter 11.' Government assisted housing, to make sure the people paid, since he was not around to collect. The people moved in with a handicapped child, 'welfare plus.' The house was made to accommodate them—(up to spec). I did many of the repairs myself. The occupants were caught falsifying documents after a police drug raid and the Government stopped paying. The squatters were already moved in and were not going to leave this paradise, and not paying a dime. The police had their hands tied as the house guests destroyed the property and each month put him deeper in debt until the only thing left was to sell the house at a huge loss. The house was run down and trashed. With the awful problems of the recession it was sold at a rock-bottom price barely enough to break even, just moments before foreclosure. His Mom couldn't get in contact with him to stop it. The dread just kept piling up. Not to mention his beloved feline passing, and his Mother's cancer diagnosis'.

His long awaited but unexpected Return Home

The last few years since he has been back he has come to my home for Christmas and Thanksgiving. He comes over plops on the couch plays with the dog and cat like he's been coming forever. He is now a big part of the family, a bonding of sorts, he feels to me like a younger brother.

It was two more years before his attempt of a tennis comeback and it was a whirlwind of a season back. His first year home he couldn't hold a racket, being so weak. He couldn't drive or ride in a car without vomiting from car sickness . . . He couldn't eat solid foods or any kind of spices. Thin as a rail, pale and easily burned. Worst of all were the reoccurring nightmares every day, along with blaring migraines. How can anyone take this and still function.—Dave was but a shell of himself.

I had been anxiously waiting for his comeback for so long. He was totally out of tennis shape and only played with me *twice* in the two years he's been back. The first time we had gotten together was a week after his return and we hit a few tennis balls. Keeping it simple just practicing enjoying the moment. Dave was exhausted but delighted to be playing again. As we were parting ways Dave boldly states, **"I thought you would be better, I was surprised I won that many games off you."**

Excited to be reunited we made plans to get together the following week. As you should have guessed, Dave didn't win a single game this time, and I took great pleasure in making him run. I wanted to show him how much I had improved, but instead he only saw how bad he was. This was supposed to be my time to shine. Instead of getting praise from Dave for my great skills. He avoided tennis completely that summer. A lesson learned the hard way. Depression does awful things to your mind as well as your body. I had taken away all his pleasure from tennis and replaced it with inadequacies. A place he didn't need to be.

But now he has sworn to practice and give it his full attention. As it worked out we practiced several times before the season deadline and I was optimistic for us going forward. The odd part was he was better than before. He revived his speed and enthusiasm, but now he had wisdom and a sharp mind. He usually got himself in trouble with his over thinking, now he was using it to maintain good court awareness. (It must have been that Zen B.S.)

As the season approached, he wanted to practice doubles so he came to my Monday night pick up games and was terrific. He dominated the night, and was by far the best most aggressive player on the court. Together we were unbeatable, so we had to play with different partners to keep it competitive. He can't be that good can he, after not playing for so many years? I swear I had visions of him hoisting the championship trophy that day. Proud that he was coming round.

This is how my comeback diary read;

Game #1 Super Dave and I played our first match today. (Bugbee and Lee) Dave already had an injury (a 3-inch gash in his palm that hurt to hold his racket.) We started out rough /scared, Dave couldn't return serve the first few games (nerves.) His legs were wobbly as the moment overwhelming us, smothered us . . . We slowly started to make shots, and stopped the unforced errors. We won but that was an exhausting match, we were glad to scrape through it. These guys were one of the better teams. We passed the first audition.

Dave turned 38 this year; he was only 27 when we first met. Now he's about the same age I was when we first met. I had been thinking back to his Big 30th Birthday bash, it was nice to have been invited—(the first time non-sports related.) 100s of people and a DJ spinning records, quite a celebration. His life was good back then. I had painted his portrait for a 30th birthday gift, on a small oval canvas. I portrayed him in his favorite Agassi tennis outfit, with me in the background across the net ready to play. That was the last time we really played together,—until now.

He still looks young, . . . his hair is cropped short military style, peppered with gray from his recent hardships.

Games #2 and #3 (Landers and Rosenburg)

Chomping at the bit, we waited through two weeks of cancellations and rain-outs. We finally played our second league match barely winning in **a tiebreaker.** We made a number of unforced errors. Dave was bad and I wasn't much better, hanging on by a whisker. Probably not deserving a win, but we stayed aggressive. This team didn't make errors. We had to win the point. A very intense game and satisfying win. I was so excited I stayed and played more with a friend who came to watch us. Dave had to leave he was buying a better car.

The following night we scheduled a make up. This time a couple of new hot shots, real tennis players. Dave was on! Poaching and hitting clean winners. We were in top form making all the easy shots. They had much more pace but we easily overtook them. We felt like pros. Dave played under control. He said in last nights match he felt faint and out of breath, intensely nervous. Tonight, he *was* a tennis Zen master. Very calm and controlled. I think it had more to do with the cough and cold medicine he had taken. He was very excited, giddy, talking swiftly to our opponents about this being his first time back in seven years, and what a great game this was even though the score wasn't so telling. They asked,—where he had been the last seven years? *Pause* . . . A question I longed to ask myself. "I had some pressing issues," he said, dodging an awkward moment.

(I offered to buy him a Hoagie and analyze the big win.) He was already backing out of the parking spot.

Our 4th and 5th matches
Defending Champions—(Jerry and Dennis)
We played bad, both having trouble adjusting.
They lobbed and kept us off the net, beating us quite convincingly. We took our first loss hard, they were seasoned veterans but we still should have ripped them. Depressing to lose our first match like that . . . This was a wake-up call! We weren't ready for this level of play.

Next up we played a team we had *never* lost to in the ancient past, another older team (my age.) This should be a breeze. Players whom Dave never got along with—(Ted and the league president Steve.) We had never lost to them . . . never even close. Ok maybe a few close calls. We had a comfortable lead as they came back and overtook us. Ouch! This match we played well,—they played better. My vision of the championship trophy is dwindling fast.

This was ours to win, as depression befalls us. I had invited Dave's Mom to join us. She use to watch us all the time, it was nice to see her in the bleachers. I took her to dinner afterwards. Dave had to split. (?)

Dave slipped and fell, during warm ups, broke his racket and tore up his knee, spouting blood everywhere. It didn't affect his play, but added to the drama. His wrist swelled and knee swelled I swear I could see the bone. Good thing Mom was there prepared with Band-Aids and smelling salts. They thoroughly out played us. A depressing second loss in a row.

Only a few games left in the regular season. We may not make the four team playoffs. It looks pretty bleak at this point, we may have to win all the remaining games.

Game #6 Another first-rate team

Tonight we **lost to a outstanding team of Twins**, they took us apart chewed us up and spit us out, not a chance of winning. Although we did play a fun set after the game (because the game was over in a half hour.) We won that fake game pretty convincingly but they weren't trying so hard at that point. We will now need a little luck (a miracle) to make the playoffs. A little disappointing but it put things in perspective.

The Twins later become our Nemesis'

Game #7- Saturday morning we are playing a good team. A possibly great team. A recent graduated High School phenom and his dad. Can we get them to implode? This is now a super-important game—it could mean making the playoffs or not. We did Win! We played our best game to date—cutting down on mistakes. We started to form game plans—(not just winging it)—better court positions, and hand signals.

Game#8 The final game of the regular season (a collegian.) This time the kid was better than his Dad. He had pace and consistency, and took over the net. Luckily his dad was not up to par this day. Dave played fearlessly. We won without a hitch, but if we didn't play our best, we may have lost.

We won the remainder of our games just barely squeezing into fourth place. This means we have to play the best team in the league in the first round of the playoffs.

SEMI-FINAL PLAY OFFS

This would really (in our minds) be the finals . . . If we won this game, the real finals would be a breeze.

The **Twins** (*undefeated*) they had clobbered us during the regular season. But we did have a tiny glimpse of success with them in the extra set we played fooling around. I never figured to win—not for a moment. All was going smooth, until Dave hit a great handcuffing serve. The return was a slow floater, I was at the net waiting for it to cross the plane of the net. They had been playing so solid, I had to hit it extra hard to end the point. It bounced *RIGHT INTO HIS CROTCH*. He ran into it. I don't know which one because they were twins. Direct hit in the nuts. He went down and started moaning and writhing in pain, got up threw his racket. I tried to gesture my condolence. A rather lengthy delay that created quite a riff. This was no longer a friendly game. A teeth gritting silence. No more nice-guy. This was war!

We were able to win the first set 6-4. Dave was on a high. He came to the match, sick (Flu symptoms) and a long hour drive early in the morning from the cape. He seemed tuned in. He believed we were gonna win (I wasn't so sure but happy to try.)

He kept focused and tried to get me to have fun. (Forget about that one bad nut cracker.)

We ventured through the second set as positive as possible finding ourselves on the verge of a victory. Dave was serving and told me he had dreamt it would be him serving for the match. He had something to prove as he double faulted the first point away. I asked if this was how his dream went.

Dave served two Ace's to close out the match. We Won! Dave shook my hand, and started jumping and chest bumping me. He was ecstatic, bubbling, this was the highlight I was hoping for.

"That was the best game ever," Dave cheered! They were depressed and didn't want to hear this. As he giggled and chattered of the high quality of play . . . They whimpered off . . . feeling a bit taken.

*They had been **undefeated** the whole summer, this was supposed to be their year.* I was happy, but more in shock. Dave continued out to the parking lot "BRING on the Finals," "I'm ready for the crowds," of the big pizza party. WE made it to the FINALS!!! Wooooooo Dave was so high from the big win against the Twins he immediately called his Mom and invited her to the finals. After a 7 year sabbatical from life he is better than ever . . . This should prove to be a monumentorius occasion.

We play the seasoned veterans, Two time prior champions; (Jerry and Dennis)
. . . **Let's get it on** . . .
This is the last big game of the year and I am glad I am in it . . . All the stars are lining up. I couldn't have asked for a better comeback for Dave after so long an absence from being teammates. He does have a calmness about him and a positive winning attitude.

This is bitter sweet—the season is over after tonight
The Long Awaited Finals are Afoot!
The crowds assembled and the game had begun. We had many chances to win the first few games but lost the first set 6-1. Very embarrassing to say the least. Dave seems to have injured his collarbone, and is in sweeping pain. We played better in the second set, gaining hope and momentum only to lose that set in a tiebreaker.
We lost—Crashed and burned.
Dave had an odd injury to his arm as he kept raising it up over his head . . . Trying to reset a dislocated shoulder or maybe a collarbone. This was a sad end to our dream more like a nightmare. Very anticlimactic. They joked about me having another partner next year. Dave was insulted demanding he was returning next year for a rematch . . . We'll see.

Well, there's always next year . . . Ringing in my head.
After having a few months to ponder the details of our demise, I am still in awe . . . No closure . . . Left hanging. No contact with Dave, he is living his own life. Perhaps I'll see him for Thanksgiving.

The story can't end with a lackluster loss. . . . An injury . . . No Highlights, No excitement! I would be foolish to think he would be around next year. His life is slowly getting back on track and he has better things to do. I won't hold my breath, but I can hope. I have my second place trophy mounted securely on the mantle for the winter. I am very happy to have had the chance to play with Super Dave this year. Having had some time to reminisce, it was the perfect reunion after all. Dave is back!

Like my friend Tom Carpenter says, "Every good adventure doesn't have to end with a championship trophy."

THE END or was it.

Super Dave and sidekick BB

DOG FOOD! An odd thing to hear someone yell at the top of their lungs. Mike was a dog guy. He didn't swear and would never have taken the lords name in vain . . . He tried to give me a yelling word. "You're a horse guy how about; H-A-Y!!" He whined like a wimpy kid that had just been poked.—"Yeah that's perfect."

Mickey J. Chwalek
the Kid from Milltown, Indiana

"It's Not Rocket Science, it's just Tennis"
Friendships aren't always without fault or flaws.

The Man, the Myth, My Tennis Partner,

Mike is a big guy, tall and barrel-chested. At first glimpse, you'd believe every story about him being an all-star athlete in his youth. A few years older than me in a constant fight with weight, alcohol and nagging injuries as well as coming to grips with his age. His demeanor is a cross between actor, Robert Urich, (Spencer for hire) and journalist Tim Russert, sprinkling in a hint of Babe Ruth. His mind racing a hundred miles an hour working out ways to beat his opponent, storing all the facts, knowing all their weaknesses. He is the quintessential Rocket Scientist, (literately the one from the joke.) I wouldn't doubt he was the origin of this joke.

I can picture him in a lab jacket with clipboard in hand, working with rocket missiles and military hardware.

He played all sports but eventually got addicted to tennis early in his adult life. Developing on his own and practicing with Lance, a long time basketball buddy. They played tennis once a week outside, rain, shine or snow. He once told me that he hardly ever won a match but the games were good, (the friendship was even better.) The Local newspaper often photographed them shoveling snow off the courts and playing during blizzards deep into December. Front-page news on a slow day, in small town, wrapped up in so many layers of clothing you could barely recognize them. Arrogantly posting the newspaper clippings on the tennis club bulletin board, hoping and receiving a couple of good chuckles.

Being left-handed brought him many advantages, but he would proudly boast to the world, whenever he switched to his right hand, "I'm ambidextrous!"—(he was not.) Not ashamed to be playing with the biggest longest racket ever made, and using it as easily as if it were just another appendage.

He was successful more often than not chasing down drop-shots, in his own words, "He charged the net like a water buffalo." Stopping was the main problem, getting back into position wasn't happening, so he would have to go for a winner. Then he would hex you with baby noises, "That's a baby shot," waaa waaa . . .

An American flag headband was the last thing Mike put on before he started his warm up routine, full red, white and blue along with all the stars and stripes. Proud to be an American.

He was very aware of his appearance, and fancied himself somewhat of a ladies' man. I saw him more as a man's—man, (one of the boys.)

In all the years I've known him I never heard him curse using foul language, but you knew something wasn't going quite his way when you heard him holler "*DOG FOOD!*" You could hear him at least five courts over. That alone would bring a smile to everyone's face. Why DOG FOOD? Good question. So I asked him. His reply:

"I'm a 'Dog Guy,' nothing beats jogging through the woods with my Goldie's, Teddy and Nugget." "And no one takes offence to it, even in church, (manners matter to me.)" "I had a coworker that cursed, 'Bird Seed,' and this seemed like a logical progression for me, somehow it stuck." He related a severe incident at work, where he upped the curse to the next level, "SON OF A DOG FOOD!" His colleague realizing the problem immediately responded, "PUPPY CHOW!" Tension diffused.

Lance joined my group first and Mike tagged along. We soon found out Mike was quite good but clashed with the many personalities on our team. When he partnered-up with me I could coax the best out of him, and his best was really good. In the heat of battle Mike was the soldier you wanted next to you in a foxhole, his heart was solid purple, that alone inspired me to push myself to the limit (in our minds we were at War.)

While I was serving he would stand extremely close to the net slightly crouched, and poach any weak returns. If the ball was anywhere near him it would be an easy point for us. He jokingly called his over head smash the 'Tomahawk,' as he slashed down on the ball with both hands gripping his racket like an axe handle, (he was more Paul Bunyan than an Indian.)

Mike hit tons of winners off the side of his racket, which earned him the nickname "framer." Raising his hand in apology for a lucky bounce was never a thought. He swore he did it on purpose and because of that deserved any point he earned, (he made a believer out of me.) Still to this day **any miss-hit _winner_ became known as a "Chwalek."**

He hated to hit a slow second serve so he tended to double fault a bit, *he was a man*, and he wasn't going to push in a sissy second serve, unless, it was—'*game point*.' I tended to double fault once or twice a game myself; it was probably not our best team strategy.

Mike's favorite part of tennis was the 'after-match sit downs,' lots of beer, and lots of statistics. Who played whom, how many games lost or won, you name it, he was the king of stats. Mike was a talker a very social being, he would praise your good qualities, but he also loved to remind you of any of your flaws, in my case according to Mike—'I had the mother load.' He especially miffed on my ever changing hair color, but he always seemed flattered that I requested to play with him, this, he rubbed in, like a badge of honor. I believe it made him feel needed, wanted. For me, he made the game important.

The Nationals

We played several times together in local tournaments and USTA team games. In a couple of seasons, we earned a spot in the National Championships, in Arizona. There he would stop and look around at the mountain landscapes, even while we were playing, and just radiate pure joy, breathing it all in. That made me appreciate the magnitude of our journey much more. He colorfully described the tennis grounds in Tucson as an Olympic Village, with all the best players gathering together from every state in the US. The grounds and hotels bustling with athletes.

At the start of our first game, he presented me with an American flag headband of my own. I quickly tied it around my head; I believe it formed a stronger bond between us. I to this day cherish and display the photo of the two of us standing together proudly posing with our chins up, chests out, fists clinched and headbands gleaming after a rather testy win over Puerto Rico. I still carry that flag headband in my racquet bag to every game I play as a reminder of great times, waiting for the next battle worthy of it.

With determination and guile, Mike willed us to victory in the few matches we played together at the Nationals, never a breath of losing.

Male Bonding

We still play doubles together for the USTA, and for a while I took over for his ailing friend Lance. Once a week playing singles outside late at night in any weather even rain and extreme crosswind storms, that was until we messed up the court lights. Mike had a private key to run the lights anytime we wanted; on this night, the lights had an electrical short-circuit. He decided he knew better (he is a rocket scientist) and he by-passed the fuse with a penny . . . the lights came back on as we raced back to the court laughing and cheering. (For about ten minutes,) when the entire transformer overheated and shut down . . . ouch! The lights were fine the next night, but over the summer several light bulbs blew out never being replaced. Boy do I miss those late night games. Let's keep this little incident to ourselves. Officer I had nothing to do with it. Honest?

The Code

Mike is a generous man, a big tipper; he takes pride in offering his teammates and opponents a beer or cold drink after a match. It is important to him. Mike is not rich, but he must be well-off (he is a working rocket scientist,) however I am very content with my existence, but I am not wealthy. Every penny is accounted for in my life and believe me the tennis till is empty. All funds allowed for tennis have been spent for court time well before spring. Never mind rackets, strings, balls and sneakers. So buying rounds of beer for the lounge is not high on my "to do" list.

Did I mention I do not approve of alcohol, especially driving home at midnight after a few cold ones? And they go down quick and easy after a heated game. Having said that, on occasion after a particularly tough match, I have accepted a cold Gatorade here and there to avoid insulting his hospitality. Sometimes I feel like I let him down when I always said, "No."

Local Bragging Rights

Mike and I partnered-up for a big end of year town tournament. This year everyone showed up to play. Players from two local clubs entered along with several regulars. It was double elimination so you could lose one game before the finals and still be in the running, which was the case with us, right away in our first round, we met up with the area superstars . . . We lost fast, we didn't have a chance to get into the game, and they pummeled us. The weekend matches were much shorter than normal, (only one set.)

Luckily, we had a second chance and made sure we were prepared for all the remaining matches. It took the entire weekend, but we did make the finals. We were granted a day of rest before the big championship match. We were now the 'main attraction.' Outsiders expected to lose having to face the same team we had lost to earlier. The best of the best, the Malatesta brothers. I had video taped the game we lost, setting up the camera in the crowd overlooking the sunken court, a great vantage point for them and a video camera. We studied the film on our off day. After Mike got over how massive he looked on TV, he soon fell in love with his image and style . . . It gave us confidence and we worked out a *scientific* plan of action.

The Celebration

To make a long story short we won, shocking everyone especially ourselves. We had to celebrate so we took our wives out to a fancy Italian restaurant for some authentic European pizza. As the evening wound down, I become concerned. They had been drinking expensive alcoholic specialty drinks along with appetizers and fancy desserts . . . It started to add up big! I'm not knocking it; I just didn't have much extra cash. As I started figuring out our part of the bill Mike proudly announced he was splurging and paying the whole tab in my honor! What a great feeling, this guy was all right in my book. He was a special guy! I was not accustomed to this kind of treatment.—As he shouted, "You'll get the next round!" A weekend to remember but a lesson learned.

Months go by and the following spring Mike and I are again teaming up for the USTA leagues and still winning. We had to go to a club a great distance away, directions were a bit confusing so Mike offered to meet me on the way and drive together. We had a good ride together reminiscing and bragging. He was particularly adamant about certain guys that didn't buy their share of rounds, just waiting for someone else to buy them drinks. Angrily pointing out a few guy's that were cheapskates. Was this a hint?

As we head out to the court Mike suggests that I should purchase his drinks that day. I agreed as he scurried to the dispenser and pulled out a large flavored sports drink, and said this should do. I reluctantly agreed as he reached in and grabbed another saying I owed him. Well he was right he had bought me a couple of drinks over the season and I had not reciprocated. This had been building in him for some time. I was tagged and finally awakened. Mike is a good guy with a point and I wanted to make things right. I didn't want to owe him so I . . .

Last Chance for Redemption

The following week was the *final* game of this season I happily informed Mike I would treat him to a celebratory pizza after the game, "My treat" . . . he was ecstatic. I proposed, "It was to make up for the pizza he paid for last year after our big Tournament win." I was proud and relieved that he agreed. After the match, I waited for him to pack up so we could head to the local pizzeria. He just needed a quick beer first . . . I had an epiphany *I will buy him that beer.* I went up to the bar (my first time ever) and purchased Mike's favorite beer and a beer for the team Captain, that just sat down with him. The bartender opened the bottles and sent me on my way. I proudly place them on the table. "What?" It's the wrong beer (they wanted summer brew). How would I know there is beer for different seasons? Back I trudged and purchase two more. Mike was happy and wanted to party; brashly he invited the whole team to our end of the season pizza celebration! Ouch! It was pretty late and there were no takers, it was just Mike and I for pizza. (The two shoddy opened beers were not wasted). There goes my tennis budget. Of course, we agreed on the biggest, belt buster, meat lovers special ever, with extra salty anchovies 'eeeuw'. Even though we were alone the celebration was well worth it. I had his full attention.

I believe I evened the score that day and felt pretty proud of myself. I don't want to be known as the guy that mooches off anyone else; I don't need to be pegged as a freeloader.

In my opinion, it isn't a favor or a *polite gesture*. If I owe you for it.

Now I know there is a 'code' of conduct that I must follow if I want to be with the in crowd. Not necessarily the place I need to be.

The moral of the story;

"When you get something for nothing, you just haven't been billed for it yet"

The next round is on me.

The Phone call
Big Mickey C. called me tonight to ask me if I would help him install a new net at his favorite town courts this weekend . . . of course I said, "yes, and bring your racket big guy";—there was a long pause . . .

It was spring and I hadn't seen him for at least nine months. He starts to talk again and then another long pause . . . "Something is wrong." He blurts out, "I went to the doctors for a routine check up and the prognosis isn't good." Another long pause—during that moment I imagined; he will have to start eating right, cut out the booze and exercise to get back in shape again. Was I being recruited to help out?

No, it is much worse . . . Cancer, very bad cancer . . . "not looking good," he murmurs, "chemo starts this week." On the bright side he let me know he is marrying the "love of his life," something he should have done 10 years ago. I am scared for him and terrified to meet him at the courts this weekend. He is so solemn, and questioning how he will be remembered. In the tension and awkwardness of this moment I thought it might ease his mind if he knows I am writing about us right at that very second he called. He perks up when I tell him. He mentions a few misadventures that had happened between us, I assure him they are in there as I reveal a few others he had forgotten. He is impressed, relieved even. I feel it in his voice. He of course wants to read it . . .

"It is only a draft at this point," I stutter. He offers to rewrite it together.

I was honored that he called me personally and asked to see me. I haven't seen much of him since the pizza celebration over a year ago. It really makes you think long and hard about your own life. How will I be remembered? I was the second friend he informed after Lance, he really considers me that close of a friend. Mike has a million friends—I was near the top of the list.

Mike, I miss you already.

As you would say, "It's Clobbering time!"

I really miss those late night games under the lights.

We met this weekend to replace the tennis net he had had over a year with the intention of repairing it along with the net post crank. He had finally decided it was time to get it off his back porch and back into the game. It fit perfectly and tightened as if it was brand new. We stood and just looked at it for a few minutes, Mike with his arm on his hip and his head cocked to the side, proclaims us both geniuses, "It isn't rocket science," he says wiping the silicone grease off his hands and shooting one more squirt of bee spray into the posthole for good luck. He announces, "Now we have to christen it, grab the rackets."

Mike has already lost thickness in his face and shoulders. He still has an appetite but can't overdue because the cancer is in his throat. He didn't put on his famous flag headband today but I did spy a couple in his racket bag, as he forages around for a wrist wrap. We were not at war today, we were just going to rally a few balls back and forth, as buddies, best friends.

Suddenly Mike went back to his bag and retrieved a brand new can of tennis balls broke open the airtight vacuum seal under

94

his nose, breathing in the distinct rubbery smell of freshly opened tennis balls, ahh. He declares, "This new can is in your honor," as we diligently took our spots at either end of the court, and started a real game. He is a bit slower than I remembered and has a bit of trouble with the score, but his trash-talking is up to par. He said he was rusty because he hadn't played in a while, I copycat his excuse. (He had just started Chemo) . . .

We finished the set with a great deal of effort on his part; I tried to keep the ball near him without being too conspicuous. He didn't catch on, but he had a few tips for my poor strategy. I figured we were only playing the one set so I try to make it last as long as possible feeling it could be our last. He caught his second wind and not wanting to quit announces we will be playing a super tiebreaker for today's bragging rights. It was short and uneventful, a bit too hot and he is winding down. Packing our rackets and tools he offers to buy me a coffee coolata at the Duncan Donuts across the street, I first decline—pause, and wryly giggle, "Sure you owe me."

We picked a booth under the air conditioner and discuss medical talk, details and google searches, diagnoses and the many tests he had been through. None of it good, not a ray of sunshine, he glances out the window and confesses his new awareness and love of a beautiful spring day, like today. Eye's welling up with a lone tear untouched as it rolls down his cheek, this is heartbreaking for me, I can't imagine his grief. Trying to lighten the moment he jokes, "See you should have let me win," I reply, "I tried." We both chuckle and head back to the courts. It was the perfect end to our meeting, out 'trash talking' the big guy.

The courts have been a bit run down since all the cutbacks of this recession. Cracks and weeds were creeping from the net to the baseline. Mike stands at the edge of the court admiring his new net and wearily sighs, "You look how I feel, but you've always been my court." "This has always been my court!" We say our goodbyes as he stops me from driving away and says, "let's keep my little problem to ourselves," "I'd like to tell a few friends in person, and it may be too emotional if I walk into a room of people, and have to explain my daily progress, etc . . ."

I sit back in the seat of my truck as he drives off. A little reality dazed, I think of the phrase Mike uses on occasion, "It's not rocket science." I just realize he was playfully referring to himself. I feel like I had just woke from a bad dream, as I put the truck in gear, ease out of the parking lot and slowly head home.

He emailed me a short message today, wanting to see the story I had been writing about our misadventures. Again I put him off, telling him it was in rewrite . . . he laughs and accuses me of being too perfect. "Just let me read it the way it is. I'll help you rewrite it." The problem was a bit more . . . I portrayed him badly in my first draft; he had offended me and in my mind damaged our friendship. Writing was my way to send the world a message. "Don't get caught in these situations like I did, beware!" There is a monster out there! It was a kind of therapy for letting a close friend go. He turned on me one too many times, and I had given up on him rather than take a risk of be slighted again. Instead of confronting him with my issues, and giving him a chance to recant, I built an emotional wall between us. It was I who was the real ogre. Now I am really losing a true friend. As I rewrote and rewrote . . . I started to envision another lesson learned. *Friendships aren't always without fault or flaws.* It figures, I had to learn it the hard way, grieving. He never even knew I was cross with him. I still have time to make amends.
Unread, he asked me if I would read, 'our story' as a Eulogy at his funeral.

I start to catch sight of what an outstanding individual he is, and what an extraordinary friendship we have. "Mike matters." I wanted to show him how he has been an influence in my life, and how I will remember him forever.

Manly-men don't use the word love, but I can insinuate.
'DOG FOOD!!'

"When you have no choice, mobilize the spirit of courage."

'Gilligan's Wrath'

"Taming of the Shrewster"
Mr. Congeniality

Gillie was a nightmare for club owners and possibly the world's worst person to have on the court next to you while you're playing tennis. He was an annoyance, a distracter, spitting foul language and extremely loud comments and noises. "OH NOOOOOO!" was his staple yell.

He embarrassed his opponents and teammates. Throwing rackets, screaming at the top of his lungs—frantically punching the back canvas wall bellowing echoes throughout the building. The complaint list against him was a mile long. No one wanted to play him, or be around him. He was a problem.

By my standards Gill was rich (He had an indoor swimming pool). A good looking guy around six feet tall medium build, in good tennis shape, in his late thirty's. His tennis attire was not tennis oriented; he wore cargo pants and a polo/golf shirt, very neat and well groomed, but not tennis fashion. This alone would have made him an outcast at the haughty-taughty tennis clubs.

I of course immediately liked him, and wanted to protect him from all the cynical talk about him, I hoped I could help. He was progressing quickly; he had the time and money to play as much as he wanted. I volunteered to practice with him, and struck up a friendship, I found him comical, and animated. I didn't take offense to any of his antics; in fact, he didn't feel pressure from me so his demeanor was on a much lower level—still there—but not as heated. He respected me, I felt it, I actually didn't think he was that bad until I witnessed him lower the boom on someone else . . . *Oh my* . . .

He asked everyone to play with him even the best of players—he wasn't shy. Most people wouldn't have anything to do with him. In fact, it was odd playing him because of his style of tennis, even warming up with him was difficult he would not hit a deep shot; everything was short with under spin, different variations of drop-shots, chips and slices.

If Gill had to stretch for an out-of-reach groundstroke, he would slap at the ball keeping it in play with uncanny precision. With this inventive technique, he could run down almost anything. His court coverage was way above average making up for other flaws. Gill also had an uncanny ability to loft lobs over a charging defender, add to that a natural overhead slam.

He was always working hard on his serve . . . right now it had a bad hitch that wouldn't allow him to fully extend his arm. It took all of the pace away but gave him extreme accuracy. He could place it anywhere, with very little bounce.

Gill was black balled and for good reasons—he was rude—mainly about himself not to others. Off the court, he was polite, courteous and well mannered. He was a good friend.

I was in a rehab phase myself and in-between practice partners—especially ones that could play anytime at the drop of a hat . . . In the morning with just a call he was ready. If it was raining, he would reserve and pay for the court, or even late at night. We played many midnight games, no one was around to be bothered.

He was warned so many times the club owners took him aside and had a heart to heart talk. They threaten to expel him, eventually coming to me and asking for my help. I had several man-to-man talks with him, he always agreed, but to no avail. The second he walked out on the court he transformed into a Don Rickles/Genghis Khan/Sam Kinison Hotchpotch.

I would videotape our matches and give them to him, to "study." I even turned the volume up when he erupted. It didn't bother him—he didn't hear it. I insisted he concentrate on his court antics . . . he didn't see anything wrong . . . He seriously tried.

Gilligan's worst Qualities were also his best qualities:
I liked Gill,

I like his enthusiasm, his will to run as hard as he could for every point no matter what. Each swing was a crusade and every point he lost from an unforced error pained him to no end (with loud outbursts) . . . he truly was in pain. It's a reaction you would have if you hit your finger with a hammer, over and over. Oh nooo not again! However, on the contrary, he would praise any good shot I made; any winner was clapped for and truly admired. He was fun to play with, you could really read him like a book if you just paid attention, it was a pretty good suspense-thriller, ok, maybe an action adventure.

Gilligan's game was improving in leaps and bounds—playing his odd strokes with severe slices; he was beating good players in the ladder leagues. He was becoming a force to be reckoned with. I knew his habits and his weaknesses, so I still had the upper hand with him, but he was gaining on me.

Gill had asked how I could hit a hundred mile an hour serve so effortless. Oh, I had all the answers, "I told of my great workout regiment, and my superlative technique." He didn't buy any of those answers, but I had mentioned a certain exercise gadget that caught his attention (the wrist rocket). The next day he had the thousand-dollar version, to my piddily old twenty-dollar model. They were basically the same idea just a few more bells and whistles. We brainstormed our own routine (the heck with the instructions and warnings). We were going to pack the muscle onto our forearms like the pros, as fast as we could. Keeping it in our cars, next to the lounge chair watching TV, on the night stand by the bed, working that one arm every chance we could. Envisioning our massive Popeye forearm beating up all the local talent. We both went wild three and four hundred reps at a time.

Gill had a long business trip several hours on the road, the perfect time to work that arm into superb form, he was winning this race. Bragging our total counts for each day . . .

We both suffered intense lateral humeral epicondylitis, (tennis elbow).

Gill had the funds for trying out every known method to cure it. From acupuncture to every cream and wrap. Which then he passes on to me, I found the Q-ray bracelet the most helpful for the nagging pain but the final cure was just plain rest.

Which saddened us both. Stop playing! As it happens, I had strained my back, so a couple of weeks off from tennis worked out just fine. Gill had a little more trouble with the down time than I did.

As Gill alienated himself from the tennis world, I took him under my wing. Of course it didn't hurt that I was now doing major home renovations for him . . . working full-time fixing years of neglect over two different mansions, along with renovating an in-law-pad, to give him a bit of privacy. During this time, I also had a chance to converse with his father-in-law. He liked to watch me work (mostly out of boredom), asking, and answering questions. He was a retired Professor in the Philippines, a position of great honor, prominence and dignity but in the States he was unjustly looked down upon as a mere foreigner. He spoke sufficient English, with an odd accent, which took some getting use to. We had many discussions on religion, philosophy and his (in the beginning great) son-in-law Gill. I believe his relationship was strained by his aversion of American culture.

He had mentioned, while Gill was in the Philippines, Gill had played tennis and was the best player, possibly in the whole country. Outplaying the best Filipino club pros, trainers and all comers that had any talent what-so-ever. Knowing Gill, it wasn't out of the realm of possibility, but I may have *misunderstood* the Professor.

However what did happen for sure, Gill was infected with the tennis 'Bug.'

I'm sure this story was exaggerated, but it explains how he impressed the Beauty Queen, "Miss Philippines" into a marriage and a move to the US . . . That and his big bankroll. She was not only beautiful but highly educated as well. (*This was added for impact*)—I really have no idea of his personal life.—All conjecture—I have no knowledge of his **bankroll**. Let me just set the records straight.—Gill is a great guy off the court, and he does have a swimming pool in his living room! Full size, with a diving board! Let's see what we can do about his disposition.

**Let the Games begin:

The local long awaited **'SPRING TOURNAMENT'** was finally here, this kicked off the start of summer and outside play. My favorite time for tennis.

Usually this local spring tournament brought out the best players around.

This was a cheap tournament to stir interest and jump-start the summer league rosters.

I was pretty seasoned at this point in my tennis career . . . about as good as I ever was. I was in pretty good game shape and physical shape. Singles was still my favorite tennis . . . This was my year to win it all—the stars were all aligned—

Singles conquest was my goal! *I was at last,* destined to win!

The Single's tournament was this weekend! It feels like a lifetime ago since my best showing ever, but this year I had my sights on the grand prize. I've worked extra hard to be ready for this and I'm injury free. This was my moment, this is what got me through several miles of treadmill, and late night workout sessions.

My Wimbledon!

Let me back up a moment—

The week after the singles tournament, the league hosts **the Double's** tournament, success there would be the icing on the cake. My league partner wasn't available to dedicate an entire weekend to play so I decided that I would invite Gill (the spurned) to be my partner in the biggest local tournament around. Maybe I should have thought that one through a touch more. I wanted to win the doubles trophy too but more important I wanted to bring someone that would appreciate my efforts and share the high of Victory. Gillie was not a bad player and most of my tennis friends were otherwise occupied.

Gill wasn't from the area so this was his first time (I believe possibly his first tournament). A clean slate, as an unknown.

This tournament was a big commotion because it was the signaling of the new summer seasons beginning, usually well publicized hoping to entice more players into joining this summer league . . . And it did-so by keeping many players together the entire weekend forming bonds and rivalries, and sparking new doubles-partners interest to join. This also brought new members to the club,—well worth the effort.

This had worked for years bringing players from far away to fight for the coveted **Silvers Trophy** played at the lavish local tennis club. Two beautiful outside courts with a spectacular viewing area above the court.

However, this year something was wrong—no advertising, and very little effort went into this years set up. The club was changing hands and the people running it had left for greener pastures . . . The sign up was lame if they even had a sign up and the price to enter sky rocketed for no reason—I suppose the people running it didn't want to work for nothing.

With a deleted roster I was a shoe in for the coveted single's trophy. The one that had eluded me for so many years. I was actually seeded #1 with a bye in the first round. I had it made.

Nevertheless, there **must be a twist** and that was my buddy Gill.

While signing up for doubles of course Gillie boy wanted to sign up for singles too! Why should I care, I have never lost to him.

* Singles tournament Starts today!

We started out with a bang. Gill won his first three matches easily, leaving a wake of pissed off people complaining of his poor etiquette, odd strokes and vile outbursts. He didn't make many new friends here. Winning the rest of his matches it looked like it <u>could</u> boil down to Gill versus me in the finals, and Gill had defeated some of the leagues best players.

I also won my matches easily. All going as planned,

I just had to beat one more player to meet Gill in the finals and battle for my ultimate Crowning of glory . . . I had only one roadblock in my way.

This was a newcomer (Jordan) a young good-looking kid, no one had ever seen before. It seems he was on hiatus from college, (Spring Break) home to see his parents.

They decided to team up (father /son) for the doubles tournament. They hadn't played together in years. Jordan figured he would give it a go and also play singles the week before as a warm up for the doubles.

With the poor turn out the director welcomed any new comers even if it was a last minute entree. Last second was more like it . . . and of course he was in my half of the draw. He hadn't played for a while, his Dad told me, as we watched him dismantle his first three, "deer-in-the-headlights" opponents. I knew his dad well, he was a very prominent fixture on my mixed doubles team with his wife (also a very good tennis player). As I recall they would brag about their son and daughter's college tennis careers. It's all coming back to me now, like a bad nightmare scene, from an 'M. Night Shyamalan' movie. He had picture perfect volleys, a hard serve and a forehand to die for. That he usually hit right at you, especially if you ventured to the net like I did. He might not have played in a while but back when he played everyday, watch out!

Now I was going to see it first hand. There goes my trophy chance slipping away. I was going to have to be at the top of my game to beat this kid, bringing all my maturity and game savvy, and hope for a melt down.

Just a nine game pro set, (the first player to get nine games wins) so if I could get a good start just maybe he would get frustrated and implode.

That was the best game plan I could come up with.—So be prepared and start fast all guns blazing.

It was working; my nerves were good along with my serve, and coming to the net bothered him as he tried to hit through me. I was up to his pace, and I was winning. I even broke his serve (more due to his double faulting and unforced errors, or maybe it was me forcing him to go for a bit more.

I was ahead and rushing, hoping he wouldn't catch on fire . . . up 7 to 5 that's right two games to make it to the finals—and—I don't know if I melted, or he purged—but he evened the score at 8-8.

I had my chances to win,—several in fact, but he was warming up to the challenge.

Now we had to play a tiebreaker—my whole tennis existence down to just this one tiebreaker. The ever so scary tiebreaker.

This was big for me, this was who I was—and why I had put so much time into my game. Being the only game left for the weekend, the players had stayed around to watch us. This was now being touted as the match of the century. (*mostly by me*)

The old man against the young buck outsider, (*not that I was that old.*) This match made me, the last chance for the regular local league guys to save face. (I instantly became an insider), and they were all cheering for me! Except Jordan's Mom and Dad, and even they liked me. Of course, I trailed the entire tiebreak but kept it close hoping to see Jordan wither under the pressure.

I had to win by two points—just two points in a row and I was there!

Back and forth, each having match point on our racket several times.

I am sorry to have let my fans down on this day. I wasn't use to having so many people cheering for me, feeling the exhilaration of each point along with me. The entire place was thwarted with one mighty swing. The oxygen was sucked out of the court, as everyone gasped and held it in. Total silence . . . I had lost . . .

Suddenly the energy skyrocketed and everyone erupted cheering us both for such a thrilling game. I had earned their respect and sympathy, gaining many knew friends including Jordan . . .

—The excitement of this week brought on several new teams begging to sign on for a chance to experience this high again. Especially when everyone gathered for the Single's Finals that next Tuesday night, with the now heralded, "**Jordan against my unanimously damned buddy Gilligan**. Both new-comers, but now we all felt we knew them.

I of course felt Gill was in serious trouble.—He had never defeated me, how could he compete with Jordan? However, I never let on, and we trained together working out every flaw and scenario possible. I had found a few weaknesses in Jordan's armor and we developed a game plan.

Jordan was a quiet self-controlled person, kept all his emotions in, dignified, and of course, his Mom and Dad were watching so he wanted to make them proud. His Dad was a very distinguished and proud man in his own right. Raising his son to respect the sports. Naming his son after the legendary Michael Jordan.

Gill was an outcast, an extrovert—Not a care in the world—he could have cared less for the trophy or the crowd, he didn't want admiration or new friends—winning wasn't that important either, this was just his latest mission. Brash, abrasive, loud and embarrassing, especially compared to Jordan. My guy was the bad guy in every way, and I was counting on it. Ahhh! Oh nooo! You would hate to be losing to such a goober. In front of everyone, but my goober didn't care, he had only one purpose and he was in the best playing form of his life. He was ready and Jordan had no idea what he was in for. An all-out screaming assault. Ahhhhhhhhhhhhwwwwww! Shit!

Jordan won easily . . .

Gill used the whole shebang. He was even louder:—broke two rackets—fell and drew blood twice gave everything he had and still didn't stand a chance—Jordan's pace alone was too much for Gill. A very limp ending, considering my big build up.—

However, the story did not end there.

It was just one short week to prepare for our revenge,—"The **Double's tournament.**" Word had gotten out that this was the **last** tournament ever in town and the entrees were tripled even with the gouged prices. My only conundrum was Jordan had his father as a partner, a great player especially at doubles, and I had Gilligan.

I liked Gill but he was not a doubles specialist. Doubles wasn't good for his game or technique. Several great players, last minute, had asked me to team up with them as the weekend approached but I was committed to Gill. "Why?" I wondered, he really could care less.

—Let's give him a chance.

Yes, we struggled through the first few rounds but hung on. Luckily, we had a good draw since we were seeded pretty high we didn't have to play the better teams until the second day . . . We hadn't played doubles together before but it didn't take long to gel. Most of the players knew me so they kept the ball away from me as much as they could, but that gave me opportunities to poach and ad lib all I wanted. I realized that when Gill served slow it made it tough on the receiver because they were concentrating on me instead of the ball. Gill was a lot better at doubles than I thought.

So we worked out our inadequacies. Plus we did a lot of switching and Australian formations, anything to cause a disruption. It paid off with these shorten matches. This took us all the way to the Finals against you know who; Jordan and his Dad. They had ripped through the competition juggernauting their way to us. And the biggest match up of the Millennium.

Of course, we had to wait until the following Wednesday night.

I felt I was at a bit of a disadvantage but glad to have the chance to redeem myself.

The word went out and the crowd gathered for a private party at a posh country club. 'BYOB'—Bring on the beer and let the mayhem begin and the beer was rampant.

This could have been the most important contingency in the summer leagues future. This little get together weekend sparked an incredible interest, in what was a league in jeopardy.

Should I keep you in suspense—will you forage ahead to see the results—turn to the final page to see me hoist the trophy while sitting atop of Gill's shoulders . . . Oh noooo

Yes, we won!

Gill had the game of his life. Oddly enough, Gill stopped the swearing and loud outcries. He didn't break his last racket, he played in silence fist bumping and hand slaps but never a peep. This time I didn't ask him to change. I only realize now he was tempered down this whole weekend playing as teammates. His confidence was boiling over.

He just finally felt at ease with himself proud of his accomplishments, he was a real *tennis player*. The mistakes didn't hurt so much when you had a partner to back you up. He had finally gained respect for himself. That is so cool. I have it all on video, watching it several years later it is so obvious.

I played very few times with Gill after that day if any,(I can't recollect.)

I believe he still plays but I kind of lost track, I trust with his new found confidence he would be welcomed anywhere.

I heard Roger Federer was nasty on the court as a youngster. It just takes some of us time and confidence to mature; we all have a different path in life. Gill's path has joined the main stream, I hope. From what I've heard, he would give me a run for my money if we played now. I'll bet he's solved the hitch in his serve, and learned top spin. Maybe even gone back to the Philippine Islands and started a tennis program for the kids, with his **beauty queen** and retired **Professor**. (I think that would make it Gilligan's Isle.)

That is a great ending. Yeah that's the way I want to envision Gill.

—Oh Noooooooooo that makes me the **Skipper.**

This final year the grand trophy was deluded to a piece of paper slid inside a clear plastic folder. I still have it. (Somewhere?)

It's one of my,—most *cherished?* The end. Woooooooooo . . .

MD

PS; My deepest most heart-felt condolences,
hearing about Sonny Jr.

The "Hitman" cometh

The Best of the Tennis Diehard practice partners
Diehardisms

Die-hard refers to certain friends you play tennis with, you play for hours at a time just to be playing. You don't have to be evenly matched. You strive to win but the score doesn't really matter when you're finished. It's not counted on your permanent personal life record, and you can always bank on another game next week.

Some guy's you play with, beat you every time, no matter what you do you simply can't win. Others, you're just that much better than they are, but it doesn't matter, you fit right, the games flow, no head-games and you enjoy every minute. You play hoping today will be the day you finally break through and win, or you play knowing you're going to win so you can enjoy the game without a care in the world, *until the score gets a little too close.* I've been on both ends . . . and I love it. At the end of each set, you shake hands, there's a pause and someone always says, "Are you up for one more set." Take a sip of water, tighten your headband, march to opposite sides of the court and start fresh. These are the guys I want as my tennis doubles partner. Teaming up with them for doubles is what makes tennis much more fun for me.

Chris Knapp was one of the best (true Diehard) sparring partner I could ask for. He was older than me and much slighter in stature, a quiet man with a distinct Abe Lincoln goatee. Always very serious and polite, with a lonely aura about him. This guy loved the game. He would study tapes, books, games on television and his opponents. I loved his dedication.

He wasn't married but he had an adult daughter in a far away state, that was about all I knew about his personal life. (Maybe I'm not such a good listener after all). No idea what he did for work, it was all gibberish to me, way beyond my comprehension. He could have been a hit-man for all I knew. That actually fits in this scenario. He did travel a lot.

I was a much better player, possibly a whole rating step higher, but our singles matches were long and competitive. I used the time to work on ground strokes, serves and volleys. I enjoyed the time, and I knew he took pleasure in the competition. He wanted so much to improve, and he did.

When I say we played for a long stretch I am not kidding, 3 hours would be a short day for us. We even videotaped our matches and studied the results. He wanted to play with the big boys, no matter what it took, and I wanted to help.

I always chose Chris as my partner for the late night pick-up games at the club. I enjoyed helping him win against all the other chuckleheads that picked on him. I sort of took on the nurturing mother hen roll. He quickly discovered to whip the ball instead of muscling it to gain greater pace, and figuring out how to use the opponents pace against them, doubling his own.

We didn't talk much before or after our tennis marathons, it was the playing together that we enjoyed. No trash-talking, no whining, no stalling just step up and play. We both knew the score didn't matter when we were done as we would just shake hands and bid each other a polite, "see ya next week."

This went on for a couple of years, and helped hone both our games. He did break the barriers of the club tennis leagues and played quite well with the better players. Enjoying every moment every play and mostly relishing every win. He could win; he just needed a few breaks in the right places . . . Don't get me wrong, he was a good player, he just wanted to play up. (Play a level above his ability). I believe he would have always played up no matter what level he was.

He was invited to play for a senior USTA team, and they even went to the Nationals in **Vegas.** That was a thrill for him, but not as much as when the USTA pushed his rating up. This was where he wanted to be, and he had finally earned it.

That winter I had taken some time off from tennis to heal a few nagging battle wounds and lost track of him for a while. As spring approached, I gave him a call and left a (play-date) message. No call back! No one had heard from him in some time.

A few weeks flew by, and I was throwing a birthday bash, celebrating my big fiftieth, and I was searching my phone books to see who I might like to join me. It was a good excuse to call him again for an invite.

Not expecting him to attend, we never really talked much socially. I went to the tennis club for any info they might have. They gave me an old e-mail address of his but they said he never responded to them through it. I sent the invite not expecting a response. Was he sick?

A few more weeks had passed, and I had changed my mind about the birthday celebration, 50 was nothing to celebrate, I didn't want anyone to know I was that old, (like they didn't.) So I had put a stop to the party. Maybe just a little late, my wife had already rented a hall and sent invitations she wasn't stopping now, but she led me to believe it was off. What a surprise, it was exciting to see all my tennis buddies, of course none of the uppity gamers, made it.

However, my real diehard buddies did. Whooping it up with a DJ, party favors and cake, relatives and old friends I haven't seen in years.

Some time into the shindig, who saunters through the door, yes it was Chris, what an incredible surprise! He had shaved off his graying Abe Lincoln beard, (which gave him a youthful appearance). It was so good to see him and would you believe we sat and talked for some time. Tennis wasn't even mentioned.

At the end of the party we agreed to meet the following morning for what was to be our last hour of tennis together, before he flew back to his new home in Las Vegas. He had had a few problems that he didn't share with me. Just packed up what he could carry and flew to Vegas cutting all ties with his past. (I was one of the casualties). Nevertheless, he couldn't resist flying back to tell me what all those hours together meant to him, in person. That's a birthday gift hard to beat. He felt he owed me that much, I was touched, and saddened. Happy to hear he had followed his heart, to Vegas (Tess, his occasional mixed tennis partner had to move out there for health reasons). Tess was a beautiful woman; just imagine

Venus Williams at fifty, including her tennis skills and height. It was an odd but perfect pairing.

Chris is engaged in multiple tennis leagues and new work ventures. I have to believe him; he looked great, he had a healthy tan with meat and muscle on his bones. (It seems he may have bumped into her, [on purpose] while at the Nationals).

I never did hear from him again, except for a small package that arrived months later, it was a videotape. Edited highlights from the home movies we filmed of ourselves playing. Over the highlights, he narrated and gave me tips on how I could improve my game, in his words, "Take it to the next level." With a humor, I had not seen from him before. Very impressive and remarkably professional, I did not know he had such a brilliant speaking voice. When we talked, I could barely hear him, and he seemed so shy. At the end of the video were scenes of Vegas his new home and lovely new wife. I still send him Christmas cards every year (using the return address on the package he sent). I don't know if he gets them, but I do feel he is safe and happy, and I helped him get through a rough part of his life. (I am guessing about that part.) He did tell me once, "When he moves forward, there was no looking back."

Chris, thanks for being my Die-Hard tennis sidekick.

PS . . . Chris **may** be a fictitious name, changed to protect the innocent and unknowing.

His wife and residence may also be fabricated To anyone concerned I have also deleted the Xmas card and email addresses.

112

The hat and beard were superimposed to hide Chris's true identity.

The Second Coming of
'Mark Adonis'

The Meek Inherits the Earth   'How Great Thou Art'
A "Cock and Bull" story

Mark was just better than I was, and he was indeed an all-around good kid.

Taller than me, younger, in outstanding shape, fair-haired, blue-eyed, with a mod teen movie-star haircut. He would have been perfectly cast in Twilight or as a young loincloth 'coming-of-age' Tarzan. California bred and raised in a home-schooled spiritual commune.

Mark was ultra religious; he worked with children, for a local Baptist church, along with donating a percentage of his pay to the congregation. He even sang lead in the choir. A natural-born athlete to my forty-year-old struggle to stay young. I wanted to hate him, but he was so damn captivating. It wasn't an act.

It was the outset of what I'd hoped to be a great summer, and I had taken the morning off to play tennis with my wife at the local YMCA preparing for an upcoming league. Mark had just moved to town, bored and lonely. His parents had recently gone off to do missionary work in Africa.

It was a beautiful sunny morning, and he found his way to the courts to practice his tennis serve by himself. My wife and I were on the only other court. We cordially said our hellos as we continued to practice among ourselves. Sneaking a peek at this kid hitting remarkable serves, three in succession, then chasing them down and repeating the process from the opposite side, time and again. We had just completed our second set getting ready to start a third, when we decided to ask if he would be interested in joining us. He was ecstatic with the idea, being a bit bored practicing by himself. He took us both on, and he won easily, politely dismissing our praise for a game well played.

That was my first meeting with Mark.

We exchanged phone numbers and arranged time to play singles before work a couple of mornings the following week.

Playing Mark was odd for me, I lost every time. I would just be about to triumph, and somehow he would pull out a victory. I had the impression that we were evenly matched but this is how our games went the entire summer. Mark was truly a mystery to me.

I had a remodeling business and invited him to work on a rather tough job I had been struggling with. I couldn't pay him much, but he still agreed to join me, mostly out of boredom. He was a better worker than a tennis player. I had to pay him extra, he was doing all the hard work with a smile. I've had many coworkers over the years, but I always seemed to end up doing the most difficult parts of the job at hand. So this was a welcome diversion. He became a permanent fixture for the whole summer, building, painting and restoring homes.

He appeared honest and naive, (there had to be a catch).

Each day for a week we passed an old client's home on the way to our current job, I would mutter under my breath, "they still owe me money," (for rebuilding their rotted stairway last year). Mark finally asks, "Why don't you just ask for it, if they owe you?" I hemmed and hawed, "I already gave them the bill." I was too shy, (afraid of confrontation) to ask again; I had let too much time pass.

That night I received a phone call from that client questioning me about the payment for the stairway repair; apparently, a young man speaking on my behalf stopped over and was demanding payment. They had been away last summer on vacation and never received the bill, or the old standard he thought she paid it, she thought he took care of it, or they just plainly forgot about it. I was shocked and angry even a bit embarrassed at first as they cursed me for not telling them in person. I apologized explaining my dilemma and ended the conversation under good speaking terms along with another job offer to build a customized shed.

I had mixed emotions about the whole deal, and pleaded with Mark not to attempt that again, as I thanked him for the lesson in bravery. I split that check with him partly because I would not have gotten it without him but mostly, because I really should have been paying him a better wage. His excuse, "I felt your grief and anguish every time we passed the place, and I wanted to 'make it better.' It wasn't being brave it was just letting them know there was a problem. I was taught to face my fears head on." A pretty clear philosophy; his parents taught him well. That could have gone haywire and caused me a lot of problems. However a needless weight lifted off my shoulders.

We became good friends, he even joined my volleyball team, and of course he was the best player. He grew up playing volleyball as a daily California past time. We easily won that championship.

He worked with me through the summer heading into the fall. I even took on a few roof jobs, why not, he did all the hard work. I felt like his older brother, though he was young enough to have been my son, if you didn't count his good looks, height and singing voice, and that church going thingy,—definitely not my son.

We played plenty of tennis that summer. Our favorite local town park court was hidden from the main road with plenty of shade next to a frog pond. It had a road-rough **tar** surface, and we had to rig wires through the net to hold it in place, (the local roller skaters pulled down the nets for their hockey games). We even had to repaint the lines that had faded away . . . However, the worst part was when the town decided to upgrade and put a coat of driveway sealer on the surface for protection, which caused an oily mess with the balls and sneakers, and even coated our hands. We eventually had to abandon those courts to the oil and skateboarders, as they brought giant ramps and stored them on the sidelines.

Writing these stories reminds me of an amusing anecdote that delves into the mindset of Mark.

We were starting a kitchen-remodeling job. Each morning the customer would jaunt into the kitchen in a loose barely tied bathrobe, sitting hunched over holding his coffee cup with both hands, in a trance sipping his coffee, staring at Mark. Mark was an incredible specimen; I could only like-in-it to a young Marilyn Monroe, coming to your house vacuuming your rugs.

Anyway we didn't catch on right away. We didn't know they were gay at the time.

During the day while we were working, several men would stop by and visit for about an hour at a time. A couple were from the local fire department . . . which was boldly written across their skintight t-shirts, and tighter spandex shorts. It reminded me of that one house in the neighborhood all the kids would hangout after school.

As we prepped the walls for demolition, we came across some dirty magazines on the fridge . . . Mark was snickering as he showed me . . . However, they weren't girlie magazines. Mark laughs as he shows me the first cover and reads aloud the title "BIG BUTT MIKE." "I didn't know you were a model Mike," giggling uncontrollably. The second title was funnier until you saw the explicit photos . . . very shocking . . . it sent a chill up my back, as I quickly swept them aside. Realizing they must have put them there on purpose,—they weren't there yesterday.

The giggles turned to silence as we began to comprehend the predicament we were about to witness. Another two young men entered the house greeted us and preceded to the back room, where we heard grunts and groans, shouts and swears accompanied by loud music.

We both were getting somewhat uncomfortable.

A minor problem had arisen, we needed the power shut off for a short time to remove some electrical outlets. We needed to speak to the owner, but he was otherwise occupied.

I teased Mark into going in the back room to get the owner. He shouted from the doorway,—no answer—they couldn't hear over the blaring music. I reminded him of his parents philosophy, "face your fears head on," as he valiantly ventured to get permission to cut the electrical power. Mark forced himself to peek around the corner, not wanting to interrupt a personal moment . . . Thank the heavens.

They were only playing video games. That was close . . .

The house looked out over a lake, and Mark had a hankering to swim out to the island a few hundred yards away. It was sweltering and humid, Mark had removed his shirt as the work took us outside replacing the kitchen windows with a giant picture bay window.

Mark drew a crowd, he didn't notice, but they kept coming up with questions for him. Eventually offering a speedboat ride around the lake. He had never ridden in a speedboat, and he was determent to see what was on that island. I warned him not to go, but they were convincing.

He agreed to go with them after work that day. I teased him several times during the day, but he couldn't resist the offer. They all piled into the boat and sped across the lake. I felt a little left out as I watched them circle the island several times at break-neck speed. Mark was screeching like a little girl, along with the captain and crew. They were all having the time of their lives, it reminded me of a carnival roller-coaster ride. (I hope Mark is a good swimmer too).

Coasting into the dock, they were all very chummy, as if they had known each other for years laughing and high-fiving. Mark had a glorious ride. We both came to realize they really were just normal people. We had let our imaginations run away on us. There was no plot to bring us to the dark-side. At least I hope not. The job ended on a high note, Mark kept his virginity, and we got paid, with a hefty tip for Mark, and a few funny stories to tell, oh, and new nicknames "pretty-boy" and "fat-ass Mike."

I never really cared for my nickname, I hope it doesn't stick.

I have worked for them many times over the years, and gotten over many fears and prejudices and grown quite fond of them.

I've been married over 20 years, and I still don't understand women. I can simply imagine hanging out with the guys, not merely a man cave—a man house—with man toys: motorcycles, speedboats, fancy cars, loud music, Barbeques, burping and farting, beer and cigars. It reminds me of my high school football years, the camaraderie and smelly, sweaty locker rooms.

Ok it sounded pretty awesome for a minute—(But that merrymaking part really puts a dampener on the whole idea). All in all, maybe I could just visit for the good part. The grass always looks greener in the neighbor's yard.

Mark took on another job over the winter with Equinox (aka Amway) along with his church chum Phil, (also a tennis player). This was exciting for Mark, he did very well with it jumping in with all his resources; he was convinced this was his ticket to wealth and happiness. I declined the invitation to join his new business venture, but his enthusiasm for the company was overwhelming, so I went to a seminar. I did end up buying many of his products; of course he was also a great salesman.

Mark met a Mormon girl from Pennsylvania fell in love, and before I knew it he was getting married and moving away. I did get a wedding invitation, but I couldn't make the lengthy 10-hour ride there, my wife just had back surgery. I sent a gift and best wishes, but didn't hear from him for a few years.

I always wanted him to know how good I had become at tennis. The championships I had won and the trip to the nationals, partly because of him making tennis enjoyable. Lighting the competitive bonfires.

He would have been very proud of me, as I am sure I would be of his life. I predict he will become something special an actor or model, maybe even President.

He did come back to the area just before he moved to visit his church. He gave me a call, of course we agreed to a tennis match before he headed to Pennsylvania for good, but it had to be that night. I made a lot of frantic phone calls for an open court. We booked a single court in an old renovated barn in East Providence RI late that night.

He hadn't played in a while (a routine excuse from him). I handed him my old two hundred dollar Wilson hammer racket and we jumped into battle. I was in game shape, I had been playing a lot, and I had a plan . . . He was rusty. Of course, I set up the video camera.

I won convincingly all the sets we played that night. Did he let me win? I don't think so, although it was possible. It was one of my greatest victories at the time, and I have it on tape. I ran him all over the court and played as well as I possibly could. We parted great friends that night, never to hear from him again. I have looked him up on the computer with no luck. I expected to see him in the USTA register playing at the pro-level . . . A few years later, I met his best friend and business partner, Phil (from his church) at a New England tennis event. I asked for Mark's phone number but that fell through, I suppose I shouldn't have beaten Phil that day. Phil did mention that Mark had become a teacher, and was doing well. Mark must be in his 40's by now. Facebook or find-a-friend, don't let me down now.

I found him on Youtube singing. He looks exactly the same.

'How Great thou Art'

Our First Championship
'Jeffrey Martin'

(Jeff and I—versus the Evil Frankie Empire)

Jeff and I had a connection early in my Quest for tennis supremacy. With Jeff I didn't have a reputation to uphold, we just played. Over the years we played many hours of singles. A true die-hard hitting partner.

He was 10 years younger than I was when we met. He had all the tennis skills, but lacked consistency. This I counted on in singles but worried about in doubles. He worked very hard to solve that problem. He was all business especially on the court, hardly ever cracking a smile.

Jeff was not a 'junk-baller' everything he hit had pace. His margin for error was high, he hit a very flat ball, both forehand and one handed backhand. The same for his serves, good pace little spin. Both first and second serves were the same pace, the second was just aimed safer. He chose to play a high-risk game or it chose him.

We met in a *one-time* YMCA summer league. He was starting to get serious about tennis and decided to test himself against new competition. He had just started playing more with his wife and a coworker. They wanted something exciting that they could do together.

As time went on we, (Jeff, Sue, my wife Laurie and I) played a lot of mix doubles. Laurie and I were the better team the first few years; I even custom built a homemade trophy with all of our names on it. The winner of two consecutive matches brought it home. It got very heavy with all the trinkets we glued to it, including miniature sculptures of each of us, and a full tennis court. We also had a dust-cover plaque; the loser was to put in its place while the trophy was away. I am the not-so-proud owner of the dust cover.

As Jeff and Sue got better they started to win more often, this was not a bad thing, as they got better so did we.

Jeff jumped in and joined me at the local tri-county summer league. When my regular partner was forced into a sabbatical. In the five years we played together, we won it three times . . . That's a great legacy.

The first year together we made it to the finals, but we went down in a blaze of glory as the invincible Nino and the Driscoll-kid took us out easily, in front of the entire league. It was embarrassing and exhilarating at the same time. We now had a goal that we could taste.

This is where you wanted to be on a showcase platform playing with an audience. Everybody came to see the finals. It was a happening event with the best players in the league.

Our second year together Jeff and I got revenge and somehow knocked Nino and the kid out in the semi-finals and were to meet up with the SUPER Italian Stallions Franky and Malatesta in the finals.

In what turned out to be an epic three set whirlwind of a Championship.

This game was the 'main attraction' for the big league season-ending cookout. This was a major happening, a yearly gala that was well looked forward to by all. Featuring great food, awards and entertainment.

It went something like this:

We started badly. In front of the whole league, nerves got the better of us and we proceeded to lose the first set 6-1, unforced errors abound. At the start of the second set, the facility lights went out, ending the cookout and awards night early. Lucky for us the game was postponed for the night.

The following night the bad guys—Aka Frankie and his meatball sidekick brought their entire families and all friends known to man.

They were assured of a beat down; they had already won the first set, and an easy set at that.

This club was filled with even more people and they were all rooting for Frankie's team, and giving us the Yankee raspberry treatment. In fact, most of them just came from a daylong cookout across the street at Frank's house . . . They were a great crowd unless you were **us**. They would contest our line calls and boo us for anything close. Joking with us from the sidelines during the match, they were trying to be funny. (The beer was rampart). I'm guessing most had partied all day. There was nothing funny about this to us. This was war.

I only had my wife sitting alone on the bleachers, quietly cheering for us. I didn't invite anyone for what was surely going to be a calamity.

We came to play with no pressure we were expected to go down in defeat, with our backs against the wall. However, we didn't lose we played better stopping the unforced errors and stole that second set . . .

Now the game was even-steven, tied at a set apiece. The crowd and Franky were stunned, this was supposed to be easy. A sure thing! Very sobering, as it quickly went from jolly laughs to high tension.

The bad guys took a bathroom (beer) break to regroup and talk to their friends about strategy.

As they re-entered the court they requested I shut off the video camera I had at the far end of the court behind the rusty chain-link fence. They said it bothered them.

(I liked to film the games in case there is a score problem or some sort of discrepancy, in this case possibly a fight). It also keeps opponents honest. What could they be planning that a camera would be a problem?

The only thing that happened out of the ordinary was a hard overhead smashed at Franky, he appeared to be hit in the face, as he hit the ground. But I believe it was deflected off his racket. There was no red mark, or swelling. I didn't make friends with the crowd especially his wife and son (mini Frankie jr) with that shot!

The crowd grew restless and the Italian boys grew uneasy. The third and deciding set was close, we were up an early break and the game came down to me serving for the championship. At 5-4.

(Let me back up for a second), the balls we used the first night were dead, soft and spongy. **Maybe** they had opened the can the day before, or they might have stored the tennis balls in a freezer, to take the bounce-life out of them. This would counter-act our heavy pace. Or possibly it was just a bad can of balls. My mind was working overtime. So this time I brought my own balls and an extra can just in case we banged a few into the woods. It helped, in my opinion. Just before we started the third set, we had lost a ball in a heavy pine grove. Nobody dared to fetch them, it was infested with poison ivy. So I insisted on opening the new can to start the final deciding set. We all agreed, keeping the two remaining used balls as spares.

Towards the end of the final set, I had found one of the new virgin balls in the weeds at the back of the court, it had only been hit once. It was perfect timing for my next serve, an omen. The most important serve of the entire season. It felt like a sign from God. If I win this service game, it's winner-take-all, for our first ever Championship!

I started the game with an ace (the brand new unused ball just exploded off the racket and in for an ace), but to my chagrin, Frankie called it a fault. The crowd agreed with Franky. (So much for the hidden ball trick). A bit discouraged I tried to throw in a big kicker but missed. **Double faulting** 0-15; (In a panic) I double faulted again Trying to force a quick easy point.

Now back at Frankie, (Jeff, starting to lose faith in me, begging me to just get it in). Well, I'll show him and I blast another shot this one is good but Frankie gets a piece of it and muscles it back just over Jeff's outstretched racket for a winner. (0-40) . . .

Down triple-game-point with the championship so close. We wrestle the game back to deuce turning the tables back in our favor. Just two points from Victory.

Time to end this match. I put everything I have into the next serve, an Ace right up the middle, but someone in the crowd yells, "net, let—it hit the net." They all decided to replay it, being such an important point. I reluctantly agree. I'm a little flustered so I just spin the serve in to get on with the point, Frankie punches the ball again over Jeff's head backing him up, in a panic he jumps (déjà vu). Reaching as high as he can, swings and misses, he quickly spun around caught his balance, as the ball bounces up he jabs the perfect drop shot.

Frankie *had* scrambled quickly to the net waving his racket, (distracting Jeff), but in-turn he wasn't ready for the return shot. Desperately Frankie stepped back into the path of his charging partner. In a 'slow-motion' ice-capades dance, clawing and pushing to get a racquet on the ball just inches away. After the dust cleared they remained motionless for a moment with their bruised egos, drained of any will to go on. The crowd grew silent, the meek covering their eyes.

For all intents and purposes that was the final straw.

Alas, the final match point was a slow rally no one wanted to miss. Several hits with a very anti-climatic error to a great game. Exhausted we had won the first of our dynasty.

Only a single quiet applause, coming from our lone supporter, my wife Laurie.

No celebrating, no high-fives, or chest-bumps, we gritted our teeth shook hands and gathered our gear to make the jaunt up the ramp. It seemed oddly quiet; almost all the crowd had vanished. Heading back to their barbeque across the street, I heard someone say, "screw this let's roast some marshmallows." That could have been Frankie Jr.

Only the clean up crew and the director was left to award us the grand prize Championship Trophies. Jeff finally cracked a **smile** in our championship award Photos.

The best part, was making Frankie and Malatesta pose with us, holding their second-place loser trophies, (say cheese). I love that photo. They were pretty cool to pose for me. Maybe they weren't that evil after-all.

(*I have several 2nd place trophies*).

The few people that stayed couldn't say enough of our entertaining play, even Frankie admitted it was probably the best game he ever played in, at least the most exciting!

As Frankie was leaving he invited Jeff and I to come and play with his Sunday morning group anytime we wanted. He seemed sincere enough. Walking away, he paused, lifting his beer in cheer form, toasting us, "I wish you had left that camera on—It would have been a keeper." "So do I Frankie, so do I."

Ps . . . I did leave the camera on, but it didn't capture even a tenth of the excitement I felt that night. However, it sure is great to watch over and over. I should send him a copy. As I said earlier Jeff and I went on to win this title a total of three times out of the five we played together. Jeff retired after our five year reign of terror, partly his job, and partly loss of interest. Maybe his turning forty. He cut way-back on his tennis playing.

Tennis never felt the same since he stopped playing. An odd void.

Hopefully we can still be die-hard hitting partners.

FRANKIE

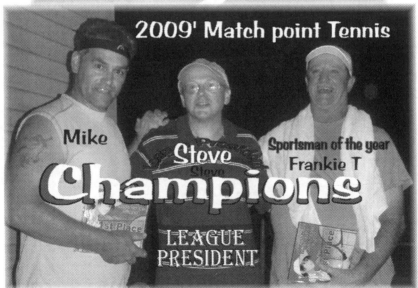

2009' Match point Tennis

Mike

Steve
Steve

Champions

Sportsman of the year
Frankie T

LEAGUE
PRESIDENT

"Frankie Todesco

"I have to eat every hour or so or I have whaddayacallit,—seizures."

I imagined him bouncing around like a windup toy
that had fallen over.
He was kidding.

FRankiE

"Sportsman of the Year"

Frank-Footer

Franklin was a mystery to me . . . We had been mortal tennis enemies for many years.

This year my tennis partner of the past five years retired, and everybody I asked to join me had other plans, and I had asked a herd of people. Tonight was the deadline for entering the summer league. I had a premonition. There on top of my list of tennis contacts was Frank. I had a vision of Franklin sitting on his beer cooler cheering loudly, watching games but not playing. Odd he wasn't playing anymore.

I had just gotten off the phone with my last candidate. He took a week to decide he'd better not join me this summer. He couldn't commit to the whole summer as he let me down easy, last minute. Each player I had asked seemed so promising. I was ready to throw in the towel and give up doubles this year. Frank's phone number was right there at the top.

I took a deep breath and called, my last ditch effort late the deadline evening.

I told him who I was and questioned politely if he might be interested in playing doubles with me. Total silence. After he got over the shock and the thought it might be a prank call. He mulled it over out loud, "You're not a bad player, Yeah, that could be fun." Apparently, he didn't hate me as much as I thought. The things you do when you're pushed into a corner.

I would never have imagined playing with the enemy. It was like Roger Clemens pitching for the Yankees—just unthinkable! I felt a little buyer's-remorse come over me as I told my wife the wonderful news. Someone finally said, YES!—She was speechless.

The season's journey had begun—Spring was in the air, and I was back in the game.

Frankie was not a normal athlete, he was a morsel overweight, in his fifties and had a crook in his back that made him tilt to the side and lean back as he walked. I had always been repeatedly impressed with his abilities as an adversary. I knew he could play, if he didn't drink beyond his limit game day, or mix it with his meds, (and he had been laid off from work, so he was home all day). **Alcohol was never a factor.** He was just normally loud and brash. I was starting to get his humor. It all seemed rather funny when I wasn't the butt of his jokes. Frankie never took the game too seriously while enjoying every minute and everybody. Maybe we created a rift in time itself, in the space-time continuum. Whatever it was, this was going to be memorable.

Our first league match was a tenacious tiebreak marathon, against a youthful high school phenom and his instructor dad. Heavy hitting adversaries enticing me to smash back ground strokes as fiercely as I could, no finesse all winners or unforced errors. We did win but it was too close. This sent us to the drawing board to upgrade our tactics.

Frankie elaborated, "I only have one request, You're a fine player but if you wouldn't mind doing this one thing for me, Please don't slam your forehands, don't go for a winner on every shot, hit the ball deep and let me help you end the point." Well of course, I was insulted, but I wanted this partnership to survive a couple of matches at least. Everyone expected we would never make it through the season together, (including our wives).

The next game, I returned every shot. I went into my backboard mode, my new motto was, never miss a shot, let them miss. The team we played wasn't nearly as good, so the tactic worked like a charm. I didn't get that satisfaction of Aces or the big winners down-the-line, but my partner was happy. When Frankies Happy everything seems so easy.

Frankie's game was, moderate paced, deep ground strokes, mostly cross-court, very dependable. A very high percentage game.

Right before our third match Frankie cunningly compliments me, "You are a great player, I have just one more favor to ask,—Don't double fault so much! Get your first serve in." I thought to myself, that's it, are you kidding me? Who does this lunkhead think he is, telling *ME* how to play tennis? You have to realize at this point I had never lost my serve the entire *two* game season, but I did go for a lot on the second serve. My strategy was every serve that went in was a point, so it didn't matter if I missed a few, I had a good serve, who cared if I double faulted once or twice a service game. But Frankie didn't like to give away free points, he pleaded, "Get the first serve in and let me help you end the point." I reluctantly agreed and made a pledge never to double fault again the entire season. Undoubtedly a feat never to be match.

On the contrary, Frank double faulted a lot himself apologizing each time. That made me smile, but I never said a word. I didn't want to put any extra pressure on him.

We went on a winning streak!

I was starting to like Frankie, he had a way about him. He told me he was going to tell everyone he was my favorite partner. Wait a minute, "not so fast pal, but, you are the most consistent partner I ever had." That phrase he liked, beaming every time he told someone new what I had said about him, and that was a lot of friends.

He felt comfortable with me, he told me nobody ever listened to him, or gave him as much credit for all the things he did do. I like to keep my partner happy, credit where credit is due.

We all play better with less pressure and a smile on our face.

Frankie labored, taking long breaks on the change over, and slow walks out onto the court. He always had something to talk about to me or our opponents, but he was always ready to go when the serve was struck. This was a new style for me and it work well for us. The younger players hate to be delayed in any way.

We only lost twice during that regular season.

Frank was in heaven, he played in another league and hardly ever won that season. He had told me of seven straight losses, but now he could tell story's of our great matches to anyone who would listen. Everyone was amazed, they had to come and see it for themselves. And he played incredible, no one blaming him, or stealing his shots. He had something to brag about.

As the season drew to a close, I realize there were many things about him that were so inspiring. He had a ton of friends that would run over to hug or shake his hand, and talk for a while out by his car after games. He was always good-natured and would do anything for a fellow player or even the opponents.

There was a newsletter sent out reminding all players to pick a sportsman award nominee. I thought, who would be better than Frankie. Frankie had my vote. It was a no-brainer.

I emailed a few friends to remind them to vote. I could just feel he would be so happy with an award that shows that everyone liked him back. That he was accepted.

Everyone returned my messages with an overwhelming positive attitude. Most players had said they were already voting for him. It made me feel good for him, until the league directors became suspicious that so many votes came in for Frankie, even players not playing him that year. The most votes ever calculated in the 10 years since the award was started.

They asked if I had anything to do with it, I just told the truth, about reminding a few friends that he was a good candidate and choose wisely. Frankie's actions did the rest.

I later wrote a letter to the committee stating why he should be the 'Sportsman of the year'. Hoping they might read it at the award ceremony.

We made it to the finals that year to be played at the end of summer season pizza cookout bash in front of 300 plus members. Frankie was awarded the Sportsman-trophy, right before the big final match. He was in heaven and they read part of my letter to the crowd expressing all that he was to the league. At least it sounded like part of my letter. It was a great moment for all, and by the way—**we did win the Championship that year!** What a season!

We had only lost twice during that regular season. We had to face both of those teams in the play-offs. Including the dreaded '**Twins**.'

Frank you deserve to be the 'Sportsman of the year' more than anyone else I can think of.

So the moral of the story is picking someone different for a partner.

Someone whom no one would ever expect.

It was a year I will not forget, a tennis journey fit for the record books and journals.

A storybook ending if I say so myself. Thanks Frankie I wish you well!

## Tennis Shenanigans

This is 'THE LETTER' I sent to the committee
Dear League Directors Sue and Steve,

I would like to nominate "Frank **Todesco"**
for the _Dick Robinson "Sportsman of the year" award._

First of all for taking a wild chance and "teaming up with me" this year.
Even, after all the years, that we had been **tennis enemies.**

Once he was assured it wasn't a 'Crank Phone' call from Nino and Bill, It took him less than five minutes, to come over to the dark side, and agree to play with me. Much to the surprise of all his tennis buddy's, and mine, he had become one of the 'Bad Boy's.' That's one of the (clean) nicknames that they had given me.

To begin with, I was pleasantly surprised, with **all** the people that "really" like him, and took the time to come over to talk with him. "He knows everybody!"

You can't believe how nicely he treats the younger players. They enjoy his playful teasing, and jokes. They seem to like him best, when he is "making-fun" of himself. They even pay attention to the sound advice he gives them, before, <u>during</u> and after the match.

Not to mention, how well he treats everyone else on the courts. Always offering to use his special can of four balls (even if it's Not his turn to bring them.) In a heartbeat, he will even give out his spare racquets, if someone breaks a string. If a ball rolls towards our court, he is the first to run after it and tosses it back with a pleasant joke, not bothered at all. If a ball goes over the fence, he is the first to chase after it.
He is always the first one to arrive at the courts.
Offering a cold water, to everyone before the match, and a cold one after.

He calls me the team captain, "Mike's the boss," but quietly he makes all the decisions, and game plans.
I loved his Frankisms and team rules:

Rule #1 Whatever you do, *"Don't Double-fault"* that's a tough one for me.
Rule #2. Get the ball back in play at any cost . . . No Nino forehand smashes.
I won't go into #3 and #4 here.

He downright enjoys being out on the courts, just like the Honored *Mr. Dick Robinson*

He is **not** the old fat guy, he likes to call himself.

He is in better shape than most people his age, and he can really cover his half of the tennis court.

Our opponents are often shocked by his athleticism, 3 or 4 times a match. As am I.

Can you believe he has been married for 29 years (maybe his wife should get a sportsman trophy too!)

<u>**Dick Robinson would be proud, to have him on his team**</u>—or to have a beer or two with him after.

He truly deserves this honor and I believe it will mean so much to him, As it did to me.

My one vote goes to Franklin Todesco

Sincerely, Mike DiGiantommaso

An Ode' to a Team

USTA Mixed Doubles

The <u>Bestest</u> Championship Season
Men and Woman mixed together—watch out!

It was a year to remember. Over ten years of competing in USTA **Mixed** leagues.

We were not your usual USTA tennis players swinging a racquet at birth, we all started late in life. We had played, as a group, for years with each other in town leagues. As newcomers we started at the bottom of the USTA league standings. We didn't have high expectations, we just wanted to compete, with a chance to win. We enjoyed the journey and the friendships.

We all admired the better players at the club and wanting to be like them in the winners circle. Maybe even have them respect us a little.

This year was different in many ways . . . I had taken some time off from tennis, because of injuries and work etc. I didn't even realize the season was about to start. My computer had crashed and I was slowly starting a new e-mail system, so I didn't receive the e-mails from the USTA reminding me of the coming season. Rumors of our team disbanding started to fly at our local club as other teams tried to coax some of our better players to their teams. Suddenly the phone calls started coming in asking about the team.

The meetings and league start in a week, I wasn't ready! I actually contemplated retirement for a moment. When you haven't played for a few months, and you hear several players are abandoning you, it is easier to just let it go. But with a sip of my ice-coffee I started to realize my nagging injuries weren't nagging so much, and turning to the tennis channel, "playing 5,000 hours" of the Australian open. I got the bug back, yes! I do want in, and all my players did want to stay together.

This year was our year. We started off strong (oddly enough) winning all those close games, we had lost in the past. You know the ones where you're the better team and you have been ahead the whole game only to choke at the end. All the tiebreakers seemed to go our way this year. Any game that was close was ours.

The team was happy; I mean HAPPY, and confident. They would come early! Jump rope or warm up on the tread mills, or rent court time and bring out several players to hit around.

On the off weeks several players would take it on themselves to reserve courts for team practices (something I had tried many years with very little interest). It really was fun. We even started to order pizza and players were bringing food for after game celebrations.

Players were taking lessons (as teams) to learn to work together, and coming up with some very inventive ways to win, using the Australian line up, and hand signals, etc. Players were offering to pick other players up and drive them to the game, and making sure they got home safe. It was a wonderful season that flew by so quickly.

We started to get spectators, teammates, wives, husbands and friends, and we would socialize after the matches. We had a beefy team newsletter written weekly telling of the battles on court and off-court antics, always with happy tones, sticking to the good things that happened, even in defeat. You couldn't wait to see your name in print and maybe a photo.

The season was finally coming to a close and we were shoe-ins, (so we thought), but we still had to win our final two matches. Not so easy (as the tension started to mount), we didn't win all the games we should have this time and the number one team had to be decided with a "do or die" final match up of the season . . .

The pressure was finally off. We didn't care so much about winning as we did about the greatest season ever, whatever happens was alright by us. Wouldn't you know, it all came down to the very last players still out on the court, as several Million people stood and watched and cheered both teams on. How do you top this? The pride of watching your team trying so hard for you. All of this was so exhilarating. Celebrations abound from both teams we all enjoyed the battle. We did it! WE WON! First Place!

What a season! And it wasn't over yet, we had three weeks to get ready for the New England sectionals, the best from every state in New England. With a chance to be awarded trophies at the Tennis "Hall of Fame" during the induction of Andre and Steffie with a ticket to go on to the Nationals. We weren't ready for this, but we craved more, as our team banded together to start a whole new battle royal.

We chose to wear the same color jerseys and made plans to make the trek to stardom. Luckily it was only a few hours away.

With injuries and other commitments, we only had a skeleton crew the first day, to be joined by more if we made it to the next round. We did make it to the next round by the skin of our teeth, with some of the best tennis I've seen all year by all teams, and it seems we were experts in the tie-breakers, no choking here.

Between the excitement, and the billions of spectators, we shined. We didn't win them all but we did win enough to move on to the next round. Even the games we lost were incredible games, marathons of players wanting to win so badly. With officials watching every move, the play was enhanced with honest calls and very little tomfoolery.

This was "Tennis Heaven," a place you want to come back too as much as possible. Special tournament T—shirts, awards, USTA towels, hats, all kinds of prizes, special Dinners with dancing and special guest speakers and more prizes, with lots of team lunch dates. Camaraderie at it finest.

Yes, "Tennis Heaven."

We made it far into the tournament, finally succumbing to the actual team that won it all (and only lost to them by a single mini-break in a third set tiebreaker). Yes we still would have had to play 3 more matches on the final Sunday (like they did) with a depleted squad from more injuries, and commitments that couldn't be broken, and a very mentally and physically tired few that remained, with an even Hotter day forecasted.

We went home that night a bit broken but satisfied. I couldn't imagine what it would have been like to stand at the Tennis 'Hall of Fame,' podium, inductee night, receiving our trophies

Or even crazier would be lining up players for a flight to Las Vegas for a week of tennis and WOW. Brain over load. *'To the Nationals'.*

We have heard folk tales from a few that have made the trip, and were still sane enough to talk about what happens in Vegas.

It didn't end there the team pride flowed over into the summer with teammates offering their home with a giant swimming pool, volleyball, and croquet areas. A super sized cookout feast with all kinds of activities for us and our kids, and more food and sweets than anyone could possibly consume in a month. This team thing is alright. With every single player on the team *committing* to joining the festivities, who would have believed that? Team spirit!

All things must come to an end I guess?

We had been a team for several years and worked really hard to get to where we were. Not just superstars showing up late for the game and leaving early, we had a tennis family, the year of a lifetime, we couldn't wait to go back to the sectionals next year.

Only to find out we couldn't even play in the same league the next year. This year the nationwide ranking push killed us. Forcing us up to the pro level. The camaraderie is gone.

I guess I will have to fire some of my closest friends whom we have played with for years and beg some super-stars to start the process again to form a whole new team just to compete. Hoping they are not the knuckle-heads that don't show up for practices, or even doubtful of making the games if something else looks like more fun that day, like raking leaves. Looks like my captaining days are drawing to an end. I really hated to lose the band of players who had been together for so long.

So I feel I am slowly be edged out of USTA,

Well maybe it's time to take up golf, or knitting.

I still have my memories of the coolest year ever.

(HEAD GAMES)

Rhode Island USTA Captain:
My team finally made it to the big time, "The Show!"

The *Tennis Club* "big time", the Big Mixed Doubles . . . **8.0**

This is where all the greatest club tennis players get together, the cream of the crop! Crème de la crème.

Most of the time it takes years of practice, and lessons, hours of ball machines, and hand fed balls. Drills and tournaments, years of districts and sectionals even Nationals to get here. However, it isn't the talent that throws me off here in the big leagues it's the mental game. This is where being *Game tough* comes to light, or the dreaded HEAD GAMES.

I've been told, "If you let them know you are *bothered,* they forge amuck fiercer and harsher." (And it *bothers* me to no end).

We have all been in a game that an obvious great shot is called out! A clean line shot taken away. That's part of the game. Even the pros looking down a few feet away get line calls wrong according to the electronic Hawk eye. Oh, I wish I had instant replay. Foot faults are a dime a dozen, almost everyone footfaults, some more than others. (How do they stop when an official is watching at the districts)?

Head games start right at the warm up, showing off to your opponent. Yeah you're good but can you please give me a ball I can hit back, so I can warm up too. Your hitting too fast, too much spin, sharp crosscourt, yes you have it all, save it for the game please. Ouch! Booming over-head! I'll be back in a minute, that one is over the fence and out into the parking lot. It's warm-ups not show-off time.

Let's proceed to the game: Why won't the server call out the score? Now and again a faint peep just before they hit the ball.

Or in the "big leagues" are you just suppose to know if they took the last close call, (or messed up the score), until they toss the balls to the back of your court and announce the game is over in their favor. It's a little late to debate any miss scoring errors at that point. Just a minor pet peeve of mine.

Could someone please turn the score cards? Normally one team has their gear next to them, a quick flip would keep spectators and players on track.

At this level what the players have picked up over years is major "Head games," they can outdo anything I have ever seen. They bring it all.

Bending every rule imaginable, The quick serve.??? They stall between your first and second serve, towel wipes, or mystery dust in the eye.

The jumping around while you're serving, or just before you toss up the ball. Ripping returns on obvious faults, making you have to chase them down or wait for them to clear their court, before you can attempt your second serve. If you hit an overhead anywhere near them, Do you get the two-minute stare? What happens if you hit someone? Heaven forbid. It's a rubber ball, traveling 50 plus MPH, someone is bound to be hit at some point.

They are experts at disrupting your every attempt at playing your game, instead of focusing on the ball, you're too much involved in them.

Could they possibly toss the balls to you, instead of hitting them to the back corners before you look at them?

Water-breaks are supposed to be 90 seconds, not several trips to the lounge bubbler, with major social discussions before ambling back out to their sides.

Come on people, have some respect for the game. Do you really have to tie your shoes that much right before I'm about to make an important serve.

Funny, I am the freak here, the outcast? My team players wouldn't dream of doing any of this, even outside at their playground pick up games. My players want to win as much as the next guy, but they would be the first to give a close line call, to an opponent. Cheating doesn't even enter their minds. They would be embarrassed if someone accused them. (Which is another cruel way to get into their heads, challenging their honor).

Integrity is one reason I asked them to join me. That and the fact that they are outstanding players. They think this is all in my mind. "Just shut up and play," they tell me.

My own teammates call me a whiner, and trouble maker. If they were to read this article they would be ashamed of me. I am truly miffed at the *state* of high-level club tennis, at least in my **State.** Do I really take this all too seriously? Use the rules, keep the honor and dignity in the game.

After you cheated me, can you really feel good shaking hands, you stupid tennis moron. While you're at it, wipe the sweat off your hand before you offer to shake mine. Possibly add a tighter grip, you are a tennis player that swings racquets for hours at a time, not a dead wet fish.

What me whine! "Anyone know a good tennis shrink," preferably a strong 4.0 with a big serve?

Special apologies to my teammates.

USTA "Big Show" Captain;

Mike DeBigtommato

USTA Tennis Rules; _'The Warm Up'_

"What it's like to be pushed up to the big leagues of Club Tennis"

Let me start off saying, "I like rules." Right and Wrong spelled out clearly. Rules are made for a reason. To keep the playing grounds fair.

I get it. The rulebook is big with a ton to read and memorize.

With this year's big nationwide push-up of all player rankings, my team had to jump into the big leagues of club tennis. Very scary for all of us.

Into the big unknown of superstar tennis, the "best of the best" of all the clubs of Rhode Island. Yes, it was intimidating and exhilarating at the same time.

Last year we had finally made it to the top of the 7.0 mountain, only to be thrown down into being bottom feeders of the super 8.0 leagues.

As a team we all decided to stay together and take our lumps, and learn to play with the big boys.

We made it to the SHOW . . .

As a captain I am responsible for my team's playing time, keeping everyone happy isn't easy. Making sure we are all there on time and ready to go with everyone knowing the rules and etiquette, of our league. Simple but important things.

We have a great league, 'Real' tennis, with plenty of time to play tennis right. Real scoring (not the generic off breeds that take skill out of the game, replaced by chance and luck). Best two out of three sets, with two hours of court time to enjoy a real battle. We are the lucky ones here. Nowadays, even pro doubles players don't get to play a full third set, not even in the finals.

We don't have to play fancy final set super duper tiebreakers, or "no ad scoring," and (No) nine game pro-set scoring. We have Real tennis.

Having said all that, We squander it, as if it was no big deal, The rules state firmly to warm up ground strokes 5 minutes and serves 5 minutes. Be ready to play 10 minutes in.

Instead, we all walk out on to the courts socializing fully dressed in jog suits. Slowly we begin to disrobe and stretch and converse, not even taking the court for the first stroke within the ten-minute limit. Warm ups become practice sessions, or one hitting winners and the other chasing down errant balls. Finally, exhaustion sets in and they begin serves. We just can't get enough serve warm ups. Not just a little stretch, we have to show our stuff, and players without stuff decide to smack practice returns instead of serving, leading us to retrieve errant balls everywhere. Time is no issue in the big leagues.

After all this, we come together for the 'Racket spin,' and more socializing, bla bla bla.

The two-hour court time, if they're lucky becomes one and a half, and now if it's a good evenly played match they run out of time and have to do the dreaded tiebreaker to claim a winner . . . On a brighter note, no one knows the new coman tiebreaker rules, (they all think they do) so the end is as bad as the beginning.

I guess the kicker is, me trying to change this life-long problem, in a new league. Yes, I am the cast out, the Jerk, Mr. Rules! I am dictating their warm-ups, and they do not like it. To them, it isn't even a problem. I don't want to socialize until the battle is over, the games mean too much to your teammates.

I have instilled a few ideas with my group, yes it will be to our advantage (but they are rules).

Up front "as Captain" inform the other team of the strict ten minute warm up (rule) being enforced, at your home court, before they get there if possible. So it isn't a shock, or provoke an argument.

Get to the court early, get your outfits together right away, tying shoes etc . . . (If you need practice rent a court for the team a half an hour before game time).

Be ready to play! Go out to the court on time! Maybe a bit early if the court is available.

However, here's a real helper. Yes, it is in the RULES. Warm up with your own partner!! Wow! A revelation!

You have 5 minutes for ground strokes. You don't have to wait for them to tie their shoes, or sipping water. Start hitting on time.

Have a routine, start close to the net, get your hand-eye coordination going. Slowly back up for deep strokes, a few volleys and a couple of overheads and your good to go. If you aren't hitting winners on your partner, you can be ready to work on your serves, by the time they have finished stretching, or chasing down all the winners their partner is hitting by them. You're ready to go in ten minutes, yes they may catch on and be ready the next time you play, but I doubt it.

It makes so much sense to warm up your own partner. You're not chasing balls, and your not nervous trying to keep your opponent's happy. You don't need to feel-out your opponents, they are all good. And we will have an extra half-hour of good tennis. Or at least plenty of time for that friendly set you play after the quick beat down you just gave your opponents. That's the time to play hit a giggle, with a little socializing, and comic relief.

Am I that wrong? Am I too serious? It is fun to see the opponents warming themselves up as they just hit winners and make their partners chase and waste time.

That could be you chasing those balls and hitting sitters for them to practice their perfect angle volley winners and big overheads.

I feel if they are true Tennis lovers, they will also enjoy the benefits, and honor the Game. A game based on trust, pride and honesty.

'It Isn't Easy Being Green'

"Mary, Mary Quite *Contrary*"
"Recycle at your own Risk"

It was a beautiful summer night, one tailor made for mixed doubles tennis.

My wife, Laurie and I arrived a touch early, to have a moment to gather our thoughts, plot strategies and scout the other teams playing.

We started warming up on an open court, (our opponents were late). When they eventually arrived the woman had forgotten her racket so off she went to beg some friends. We finally started playing our match nearly an hour late, now with a threat of darkness. It seemed every time we turned around, we were being delayed by stray balls crossing our court, or chasing our own miss hits into the woods or parking lot. Luckily, the game was going our way, because the whole evening became very cumbersome. As the game ended in our favor we shook hands packed our gear and headed off the courts.

Laurie grabbed a few discarded empty tennis-ball cans, and old water-bottles left by previous players and proceeded to dispose of them in the trash container outside the gate. Mary, (the league court manager), sprinted over to us and in an insulting manner, accused Laurie of horrendous recycling habits.

It was an unusually stressful game we had just played and this was uncalled for, Laurie is fully conscious of a clean global environment. She was the one picking up someone else's left over rubbish and putting it into the trash container . . . What? OH NO!, "You don't throw plastic in the barrels marked trash," "You must take it home and recycle." ("What the heck?")

Oh yes! She was the head of the local town trash committee and that was a big no-no! On and on she driveled, about the benefits of recycling . . . (It had been a stressful night already). We weren't

147

amused at all, just totally insulted, I wasn't reaching into the barrel of garbage and bees. I suggested she could be the good Samaritan and take the plastic home with her, it wasn't ours to begin with. Pointing at all the trash around the grounds that she could bring home and take personal care of.

It started to get heated, when a stray ball flew over the fence into the parking lot, and she took flight after it. It was our cue to disappear as well.

A few days later I was at the courts watching a friend's tennis match, when Mary pulls up a seat and proceeds to go off on a tangent about her plight of recycle. When I finally squeezed a word in edge wise, I told her I had seen a sign outside the school that said, "Bottle drive collection zone" and that they surely would have retrieved the bottles out of the barrels for themselves. So we probably did do a good thing. She thought my theory was absurd, but it was a good topic ender. We changed the subject back to the match and her son's court antics.

She really was on the town recycle council, committed to do the right thing. This was very commendable.

The end of that week I had a men's doubles match, (as it happens), with her "Husband and Son." She was there to watch as well.

Fortunately, my team won with exceptional effort on a hotter than usual evening. I had noticed her son had carried in a couple big bottles of Gatorade under his arm. I was amused to see him drink that much liquid. With the incredible humidity her husband also drank his share of water and left a few empty bottles in the wastebasket attached to the net post, her son just left his on the table next to the bench. After an exhausting match the guys toweled off, grabbed their tennis gear and left the court. She had probably forgotten about the whole incident, but I couldn't let it go.

(I couldn't help myself).

I called the salvage-lady over to inform her that her recycle-genius son left his recyclables on the table. That was a travesty didn't she teach him to be ecologically friendly. She sighed and called him back to collect his empties as she watched in disgust, with a smidgen of embarrassment. I wasn't done with my payback yet, as he walked away. I next informed her that her husband threw his water bottles in the court wastebasket. Steaming she sent him back after them. Oh, but he forgot the empty ball can, also in the barrel, he wasn't smiling anymore as he fished out the empty can and cap, He started to leave as he looked up at me, "Is that all?" oh no! "I said you brought the balls, and they are spread out at the back of the court, I can't believe you left trash out on the Court."

Needless to say I didn't make friends that day, but she was the one preaching at me!

I didn't make up these rules.

My wife, was **not** tickled with the shenanigans I bestowed upon them as I boastfully acted out my yarn of payback. She is still expecting retribution. I apologized to the Husband, with a slight explanation, he seemed to know where I was coming from, but still wasn't amused.

At least not as much as I was; Winning the payback lottery that night. How often does that happen?

I'm sure this will come back to haunt me. I probably shouldn't have brought it up again.

Oh, by the way "**Do Recycle,**" Don't leave your junk out on the court, especially the balls no one wants your used ball put them in the can. kids will find them if they want them. Show a little respect for the court and the game.

<u>Mary you are on the right track!</u>

PS.. Thank you for not getting pissed off—I can really be a jerk!

PPS.. The names have been changed to protect me—She didn't see this as being funny, cute or amusing.

In fact she has threatened to get her revenge in court—the tennis court.

—yeah, She didn't think that was funny either.

Mary, Mary quite *contrary*—

How does your garden grow?—with silver bells and . . .

What the hell are cockle shells?

My Super Score Keeper Watch

THE WATCHMAN

Did you ever have one of those days where nothing goes right at work, or at home, but there's always that light at the end of the tunnel, because you're playing tennis tonight. None of that bad day matters when you drive into the tennis court parking lot.

Well, lately it's been the opposite for me. My problems and psychosis start when I put on my sneakers and collect my rackets. My last few games have been under exceptional duress, mostly from scoring problems and disagreements. Not only easy stuff like inner game scores; (30-30) or which side to serve from, but set scores too. Even at the changeovers after just three games, I thought I'd won two and lost one . . . It turns out, they demand, "You lost two and only won the one game." Very frustrating, it was happening all too often.

We didn't have the luxury of mounted net-post scorecards to flip after every game. I was getting a touch embarrassed asking the score repeatedly. I needed to know the score sooner than just as they tossed the ball to serve. Sometimes I had to wait to see what side they lined up on, before I took my place. I just detested not being confident when I'm calling out the score.

I was at a point in my learning curve where my brain was full, and needed time to file all the important stuff I had learned. At this point it was all I could do to concentrate on short term memory: Head up, eye on the ball, split step, who's that in the crowd, is that approach good enough to follow to the net, bend knees, scratch your back, stiff wrist, point finger, etc.

Long lasting points twenty or more strokes, because we were getting better at keeping the ball in play but not yet able to hit winners, or not willing to take the chance of missing.

Games were heated, and so important to me, it was who I was, (a winner or a loser). I let the pressure take me over. I did have a small breakthrough in my fight against short-term memory, "driveway chalk," good for game scores, but I needed help during the game.

One fine day the Heavens opened up.

The most beautiful invention of modern times was revealed to me. A (score keepin' WATCH.) Oh my God! Sporty and comfortable, a little complicated at first but with a little use it was, automatic—digital—and stylish too! I would diligently press the button after every point (it was almost relaxing, like straightening your strings between points). It helped me focus. I didn't have to ask the score I just looked at the watch and planned my next strategy by the score on it. We became pals. When I look back at old video's I was always staring at the watch in a trance, as I was preparing for the next point. It was my comfort zone.

One intense moment, I was in a particularly heated match and studying the watch more than normal trying to figure out what to do to get out of the current jam. My opponent, was rather disgruntled towards me, and finally asked, "Are you late for an important date, your always checking the time?" Pretty funny.

I had other players mad at me when they ask me what time it was, "I have no Idea, this isn't a clock."—They didn't believe me.

Well, the world was back to normal for me and life was good. I couldn't wait to be on the court again. I still had scoring arguments, and believe me, they don't care what my little watch says, (there *was* room for human error,) but I had a reference to start from. I had occasionally brought my video camera and left it recording, behind the fence, to check my body language and form, even my tactics. That's when I started checking them afterwards for scoring problems. (I was being hoodwinked).

So I wasn't so stupid after all and I had proof.

All was good in tennis town until one day, (you guessed it) my super score keeper watch died. My crutch for over a year. No, they didn't make them anymore they didn't sell very well, can you believe no one would pay $60 bucks for the comfort of knowing the score. I was on my own again . . . It was kind of liberating in a way.

I can't believe there wasn't a single watch left for me to purchase or parts to fix mine. I did wear it out in just one year that might have been part of the problem why they went out of business.

What I learned from this was; know the score first, make a real effort to say the score out loud each time, so you aren't questioning it. Now *be thinking* of your next move. Focus on something . . . it calms your mind, and slows you down, canceling out the outside interference. You must be thinking ahead . . . thinking of all the possibilities that may happen and what you will do if they happen. So your game isn't; wait and respond. Have a plan, be in the moment. I understand what focus means much better now. When coaches are yelling, *"focus"* it doesn't mean just look at the other player. It means get in the game. Plan ahead in your mind, it will slow things down.

They should be yelling PLAN AHEAD! That, everyone could understand.

(In closing,) Remember if you lose,—you're not a loser in life, You're on a journey and you must be willing to take a few lumps . . . to get better. Losing is just part of the game. Everyone loses. Everyone.

PS.. If anyone has knowledge of a digital super *scorekeeper watch* give me a call (maybe by now it will tell time too) and send a text message!!

'MIXED DOUBLES CHAMPS'

The Eagle has landed   Goosebumps
'I've been Goosed'

Ten plus years playing in the same summer league fighting our way into the highest levels of the Mixed Doubles world. Silver, bronze, gold, Ruby, Emerald, Titanium, Platinum and now the highest level 'Diamond.'

They say you shouldn't play tennis with your wife; it's a sure way to wreck a marriage. That isn't so with us, at least not this year.

A local area league with a base of some 300 players with so many divisions it could make your head spin, and empty your wallet.

This was our year from the start, we couldn't do any worse than last year, and we didn't win a single match all that season! This was due to injuries and a lack of wanting to be there, pretty much anywhere else would do. Our marriage held strong through those rough times.

But this year our USTA mixed doubles team just won the State winter league and almost made it to the Nationals.

We were on a high, a tennis high and we came out of the gates swinging for the fence. We won the first few close matches then coasted for a while until we met up with the local pros.

They had just gotten back from two weeks at tennis camp. We gave them a good game, but we lost. That team was good, and the next few teams we played were even better. We went down in flames with a temporary—loss of focus.

The rest of the season went pretty smoothly winning fairly easily. The only trouble now was playing all the games that were rained out, or missed from various vacations etc. Trying to arrange five matches in the final week with more rain in the forecast was tough and we needed the wins to make the big league play-offs.

When it was all said and done we squeezed into the top four of the highest division playoffs.

The other three teams that made the playoffs had beaten us pretty easily during the season.

Being in the fourth place spot we had to take on the undefeated #1 superstars right away in the semi-finals. A bit nervous but excited.

We seemed like robots that night, on a mission with nothing to lose or prove. The old just *"Happy to be there"* syndrome. We won easily, almost too easily as they fell apart. We out played them in every way possible. They argued and berated each other; they couldn't believe they were losing to us. They had beaten us so convincingly just a few weeks ago. There was a good crowd on hand, they had a lot of followers and family watching and it made them more embarrassed to be losing. Winning that night was sweet.

Off to the finals

It was a great night for tennis except it was dusk by the time we warmed up and started the match. The sunset made for a tough backdrop to serve into or do just about anything else. This time we were nervous, because we wanted to win badly.

They started the game on fire and won the first set quickly, we were dazed. The crowd was happy for them hoping they would get revenge for us beating their town heroes; who were in the front row rooting loudest against us. The second set didn't start any better as we went down three quick games. That's when we started to make plans for ice cream sundaes after the game to ease the pain and celebrate the end of a good season. My wife breaths a heavy sigh and says, "Just play and whatever happens,—So be it."

We relaxed a bit, it cooled down a few degrees and the sun had finally set enough that the court lights took over and you could really see good.

We were set for a come back, then we lost that next game at love. Ouch! That makes us down a set and two breaks of serve, 0-4 (double ouch!!!)

I take a deep breath and prepare to salvage my serve. Tossing the ball up I pull the racket behind my head and start to recoil into . . .

Out of the dark sky above the lights there was a goose descending on me.

Apparently the geese in the field next to the courts were grazing and didn't notice the darkness fall because of the tennis lights and when they took off the young geese got confused and brushed the tops of nearby trees. Disoriented they had to emergency land onto the lighted court and me. After the confusion settled the young geese waddled around honking for their parents to help find them . . . The opponents didn't want to wait another second to get their trophy and took after the goslings yelling and swatting with their rackets, trying to scare them into flight. This didn't go over well with my wife and as shy as she is, she took flight herself after the other team.

She was crazed at their stupidity and slowly ushered the goslings out to the field and the awaiting parents.

Still teary eyed she readied herself to continue our demise, but swung with reckless abandon. Mentally more focused then I have ever seen from her. She was back, and on fire, and I helped.

We won 6 straight games to win the second set and 3 more into the final set until we finally came down off the cloud, a bit drained and out of luck . . . The bad guys worked their way back into the final third set managing to tie it up at 3 all.

Back and forth it went until it reached 5-5.

Wouldn't you know a wild rabbit jumps out of the woods next to the court and slips in through the gap in the gate and onto the playing court. (Oh no, now what?) The knuckle head opponent decided to chase the rabbit, but ended up throwing stones at it to scare it off.

The wild rabbit only knows one exit and they were blocking it . . . Up goes the blood pressure and 'the wife' goes on another tear—to save the rabbit, and shoos it to safety. By now your thinking this was what we needed to propel us over the finish line, and you could be right.

As we resume the match a pack of coyotes on their nightly trek, distracted by the bright court lights, run up to the chain link fence and start howling at the moon. OK, I'm kidding, but we were visited by another rabbit or possibly the same one just from the opposite gate . . . By then the game was over and the long awaited trophy was ours. Shaking hands among the gentle applause of some really bewildered spectators.

We both hugged our Diamond division league plaques as we enjoyed the delights of our mega coffee sundaes with nuts, whipped cream and double cherry's. *Yes, Karen, this ice cream was really, really GOOD! Did I mention mine had a fresh baked brownie inside? oooooowwww . . .*

"Champions" of the entire lot of them . . .

The taste of a long awaited victory was never sweeter.

Truth can be stranger than fiction. **'The End'**

Mike wasn't afraid of Dying—
He just wanted to live forever . . .

Michael J. Chwalek R.I.P.—Christmas 2011

A cross between suave actor
Robert Urich
(Spencer for hire)
and
The intelligent Journalist Tim Russert
Sprinkling in a hint of Babe Ruth

The Quintessential Rocket Scientist

A Year to Say Good-Bye

As I walk through the valley of the shadow of death
Michael Chwalek My Journals Final Chapter
Mickey J.—the boy from Milltown Indiana.
It is said: when you have no choice, mobilize your spirit of courage.

I was sitting at the club waiting for a tennis match to start; fellow players were talking among themselves. One mentioned he was a little tired because he played late the night before. It seemed he was playing with Michael Chwalek. Late at night was Mike's best physical time to play during his extensive Chemo sessions.

The club extended his court time allowing him play as long as he wanted, no extra charge, which usually wasn't very late. The chemotherapy has taken its toll.

I pretended I didn't know Mike was sick. (It was supposed to be somewhat of a secret, for the time being.) The fellow just looked at me and said, "He doesn't have very long," with a tear in his eye. Never explaining anything, then he changed the subject. This was very emotional for me. Hair on the back of my neck grew taut and I started to choke up as my throat drew drier.

Mike and I have been corresponding by email over the last couple of weeks; he seems like normal Mike.

We talked about his biography and some odd jobs. In about a week, I'll be going over to work on his house, in case he needs to sell it. His wife hates the New England winters, and threatens to sell the place the second he dies and move to Florida. She has wanted to move for some time. ♥ Perhaps this was her incentive for him to get better.

I have been wondering how I might help him in the future, as his cancer gets worse. Visit, play cards? Take him for a ride to watch our buddies playing tennis, a slow dog walk, movies. Maybe I'll dig up those old videos of us playing tennis, be his personal trainer to build up his strength or just be a friend.

Would he like me to send out photos of him (possibly with a beer glass held high in cheers fashion) to his friends each year upon his demise? Just a remembrance in his honor. Would he like to record a video to be sent to certain people after things calm down? Run a tennis tournament in his honor at his special court, with the proceeds to fix the courts.

Mike never wanted to acknowledge any possibility of dying. So this was not an option ever. In fact, he wouldn't quit work, or take a sabbatical; he was always planning to get back to normal.

It's the beginning of the summer tennis season he arrives at the playground tennis courts, two hours late, as usual. Mike throws on his sneakers, grabs his bag of rackets, jaunts through the gate and spies me on one of the back courts. I give and receive a huge full arm wave. As he jogs towards me, he looks fantastic.

. . . . I can't believe it . . . I haven't seen him for months.

He has a new sleeveless black spandex jersey stretched across his chest. He looks vibrant. I had to comment at how great he looked . . . Mike took that in stride as he lifts up his shirt to show off his new six pack. WOW! He has lost weight but it looks good . . . I've never seen him look so fit and trim—so good. He was flaunting it, as he bellows in front of all my tennis friends, "Something looks different about you," "Yes," he loudly broadcasts, "You've got darker hair, the last time I saw you it was mostly gray."

He repeats this many times making sure everyone hears his not-so-funny joke. It is very awkward for everyone; like watching a bully take someone's lunch money, and you were too afraid to get involved. Like a big brother humiliating his younger sibling.

He moves towards me to shake my hand but grabs on with a headlock and rubs my head shouting he was trying to rub off the grease. So funny . . . ha ha. I shake it off somewhat disheveled. He thought he was funny, but he was the only one laughing.

I watched him as he warmed up in the court next to mine. I believe he colored *his* hair, he looks great with a big smile and loads of energy. A moment of quiet sets in as everyone is back to their games.

During the pause he shouts over, "I see what is different,—you look rounder, have you gained weight." OH MAN! He's treading on thin ice here. I ignore him but he insists that I've grown in mass. I wanted to make a comment about his weight loss technique being chemo but held my tongue, barely. Cancer was not a subject for trash-talk; he had effectively thrown me off my game.

Most were leaving since we had started around five, but Mike was fresh and begs for one more game against me and my current partner *Super* Dave. He chooses the best player left to rival us. All the others headed for the parking lot.

It started out all guns blazing but soon he started to lose his pep, it was getting late and we were all wearing down. As we packed our gear, and headed for our cars, Mike asked if I had the draft of our misadventure story. (His Bio). I had it in my racket bag.

He opened the folder and the cover-sketch I made of him standing in front of his home fell out. He picked it up and just stared at it in silence. The next moment he darted for his car. He was overcome with sadness and needed a moment to regain his composure. He later told me it was like being honored with a lifetime-achievement award while you're still alive. Or seeing your name on a gravestone. A shocking reminder that the nightmare could come true.

He was amazed at the bulk of it. He somehow thought it was just an article that he could read quickly, not a full blown novel. He was rushing to join his wife at a nearby restaurant, being late he hastily thanked me for emailing him a bunch over the last few weeks and for just, 'being a friend.'

He whispered, "*After awhile I have just gone numb to the thought of dying and I am going to live as much as possible while I can,*" and drove off . . . Again I am left in a daze—stunned.

Several days pass with no word from Mike. He couldn't get past the first page but eventually he had his wife read it to him in the car driving to Maine for a mini vacation. He emailed that he '**loved it**.' Couldn't believe how much work I had done on it.

Two things; don't mention where he works and don't put his name on it.

"If I don't put your name on it who cares where you work?" I steamed to myself.

No name? It's a tribute to you—numbskull, a homage to your tennis life.

He doesn't want his 96 year old Mom to know he was married again or that he has cancer. What? Doesn't she have Alzheimer's—and short term memory loss? You're dying and this is what you think about—I am beside myself in disbelief, but nothing now-a-days makes sense to me.

He says I can use his nickname Killer Kowalski—ya that does it for me, killer . . . next time I see him he'll probably be in an underwear ad showing off his Abs. So many emotions, wow . . .

The following week

Tonight Mike showed up for the tennis games early. It was the fourth of July extended weekend. Mike had the work day off and he was well rested. A heat wave was in its third day of what was to be several. We warmed up together waiting to take on the winners of the court next to us. He suggested playing a quick set of singles while we waited. Mike looked good with his new weight loss plan but he seemed to be unstable. Mike's chemo and meds warned him to stay out of direct sunlight, (like that was going to happen).

Ninety-nine degrees alone was tough, but the air quality and beating sun was too much, Mike had to find shade. Finally we got an opponent (two girls—but they were really good). He struggled to get ready to play after sitting for a good ten minutes in the shade. Mike and I floundered, and went behind early.—As Mike got his bearings we started playing better and eventually we did win, but we took a verbal whipping for barely pulling out the win from the Girls. Mike played several games that night getting better as the sun went down, playing well past ten o'clock under the lights.—He couldn't say enough of how much he appreciated having one more chance to play on such a beautiful night. It was a great night and I, for a moment, imagined it was my final night of tennis. I soaked it all in, who knows if I will get many more of these perfect nights myself.

Mike had his Flag headband on. It made him feel like Captain America. That, I thought was pretty cool. I had mine in the bag but was waiting for a better moment to bring it out. Mike had poured his gallon jug of water into a cooler, and then he asked me if I had any spare water.??? He used his cooler to dunk his hands to stop the burning. I only had the one bottle, and it was warm from being in the truck all day. I gave it to him and he poured some of it on his headband to cool off his head. It was a good night, ending before anyone got hurt. I couldn't wait to get in the truck and turn on the AC.

I'm going to work on his house this week, (the heat wave week) oh boy.

Working at Mikes I found a ton of rot on the porch. We needed to replace all the rotted siding right through to the inside including a support beam. Mike greeted me in his underwear at the door, just after a morning shower getting ready for work. He looks good—maybe it's time to pose as that underwear model. I feel soon he won't be able to keep any weight on, (I am afraid for him). He seemed in a haze. Mornings are the worst time for him, but he perked up as we talked.

He had been reading his medical report, and announced the perfect body healing methods. The two things proven to help the human body: eight glasses of water everyday and daily aerobics. Jokingly, I said I was hoping sex to be the second,—as we laugh he says, "no, that's the third." He immediately starting his stand-up comedy routine about a man bragging of his sexual prowess. The punch line was to find out Romeo had been alone the whole time. The joke was lame but watching him tell it was entertaining. When he smiled his whole face came alive. No matter how many times he told it.

He had to get to work. All his doctor visits are considered vacation time now,—because he has taken so much time off. I ask why he didn't just quit or take a leave of absence, retire. He is still hoping for a cure and will need the job security and insurance.

Working today at Mikes.—He drove into the yard just as I was leaving. He had been at an 8-hour chemo session. We talked at least an hour; I had to cut our talk short to get to a league match. He came with me to watch, bringing his racket hoping to play after my game. I am tired and hungry and hot, but I agree to hit with him. We couldn't shake hands or touch; he was radioactive, with the chemo poisons. It was too late to play a set so we decided to play a tiebreaker. He wore the flag headband again.

Three tiebreakers and a super tiebreaker later, seems we had plenty of time after all.

He was glad to be out in the fresh air moving around after sitting all day tied to a bag of chemicals. He was moving pretty well.

He shouts from the other end of the court, "If the chemo doesn't work he is going to try—coffee enemas, every four hours," (an old wives tale). I paused and replied, "I'm busy that day," . . . we both laughed pretty hard . . .

While we were playing, the sun had gone down to a point that I couldn't see him swing and the ball was right next to me when I did see it. It was a bit tough to play in the dark but fun to hear Mike giggle. He didn't want to stop.

There was a streetlight behind me, Mike seemed to think it gave him an advantage, but I doubt it. He said it reminded him of this reoccurring dream he kept having. *As he waited for my serve, the light (which was a courtesy sidewalk light,) was right over my shoulder . . .* In his dream that was God calling to him. He stressed that I was actually in his dream. I made light of it, but I was truly touched.

Now trying with all my might to win the final super tiebreaker, I didn't want to hear how an invalid beat me. That's what he would call himself to get me going. He was beating me, fairly easily. Mike had gotten better since the sun had set, and the trash-talk got bolder. Mike seemed energized taking out his can of bug spray as the mosquitoes' hunted us down. They were so thick we finally had to go home. They zeroed in on his bleeding needled hole. There is going to be a lot of radioactive mosquitoes.

This could be the start of my next Sci-Fi book.

The next day was my last day working at his house for this project. While repairing a broken outside drier vent I had noticed it was jam packed full of lint. I went into the cellar to clean out the long dryer vents that traveled through the cellar ceiling. Suddenly I heard water dripping, more like a hose left on, splashing. Water had come through the ceiling and was soaking everything. I wanted to run . . . I didn't want any part of this . . . There was a hole in the water line shooting the water behind the wall of the bathroom. I found the shut off, called a plumber friend, and started to clean up the water. Luckily there was minimal damage, just missing the book shelves and thank goodness the computers were across the room. Lots of water entered the cellar soaking the rug. I had a wet-vac with me, (that I had used to clean the vents), to suck up the water. I stayed late and helped the plumber find the leak busting out several walls.

I went back the next day to fix the walls. As I was leaving Mike had returned from the doctors, he had just had a throat scope. They inserted a camera to check his progress. He had brought home a giant Italian sub sandwich. His appetite was still good, in fact, Mike devised a plan. Knowing that cancer patients have trouble keeping on weight, he was going to eat as much junk as possible to store up the fat. This seemed obvious to a 'Rocket Scientist,' and pleased his taste buds, but baffled his Doctor.

He was very emotional between the medication he had taken and the good diagnosis. He offered me half his super-sub. I couldn't resist his charm, as much as I needed to get to my next job. We sat and talked for several hours. Being drugged made him ramble, in a good way. He really opened up to me. We touched on several subjects; very emotional stories of his son's battle to stay alive with many prayers answered over the years.

He gave me an extra check for $200 just for the help with the water leak. I hadn't charged for the extra time that I was there cleaning and working with the plumber. I tried to give it back but he insisted, saying he was prepared to give me $500 . . . So this was a bargain to him. I told him I wouldn't cash it until he came down off his high from the drugs.

Before I left I asked him to enter a local town tennis tournament for old time sakes. He was due for a chemo blast a couple of days before the tournament. He was wary because of the chemo making him weak, his wife overheard us and was totally against it, so I didn't push it. A week later, moments before the deadline, I get the call. He wants to play.—We entered the senior, 50+ division. Luckily only four teams signed on for that division this year.

We are playing his nemesis 'Hindu Al' in the first round. Al has won the seniors the last three years and brags excessively as we entered the courts. Mike is already combat ready and wants to knock him off his pedestal. Mike looks around for a line judge to call Al's notorious foot faults.

Of course I make a big deal about wearing my matching American Flag headband into a battle worthy of the red, white and blue. We are brothers in arms.

Mike puts on a new softer golf glove stuffed with medicated toilet paper because his palms are super sensitive and blistering as are the soles of his feet. He has pain holding a racket tight, and decides to tape the racket to his hand so he doesn't have to squeeze it.

Mike was carrying a wooden crate, he found outside the courts, to sit on between games. He needed it; he gets very winded, and had to sit to catch his breath. He played valiantly but frustrated with his stiffness.—Mike knows he was a much better player as he struggled with every ounce of energy he had. Over all he genuinely seemed happy to have had the chance to play with a few shinning glimpses of greatness. We didn't win today, but just by being out there, made us feel like winners. We found a shady spot and watched a few matches, gathering ourselves.

It was time for a mega pizza celebration for getting through it all. Mike had invited everyone within hearing distance,—but luckily had no takers. I had wanted his full attention. Mike offered to buy the pizza. I tried gallantly to pay for my half. He said I was a cheap date no pay-backs required.—I gave in. I made sure he knew I had paid his entree fee.

After we finished brooding and analyzing the day's crusade. I had his attention for a mystery I want him to know about.

I told him about the Carpenters (customers that I was doing work for). Karen was a retired writing teacher, and I had asked her to proof-read the story I was writing. She was excited with my will to write and got more deeply involved, giving me books on writing and offering to tutor me after work. We really started to get emotional, as we worked together to bring this tragic story to life. I even brought the painting I did of the main character Mike . . . Then something clicked, she recognized Mike from a once a year Super bowl get-together she had attended for years. She didn't know he was sick, played tennis or even lived close by. They had a mutual friend that arranged this get together. She immediately started to grieve. From reading and studying the story she felt like they had been close long-time friends. An incredible *coincident*!

Reading someone's tribute that is dying is tough stuff. They had butt heads over every imaginable subject, and argued sometimes their entire visit. Mike loved to show off his intelligence, he *was* a rocket scientist, but she was a Harvard Grad. A worthy opponent. This last year was different he had apologized for being abrupt to her. He was a complete gentleman mentioning how much he enjoyed her company as he gestured at the chance he may not be back next year. They had wondered if he was sick or moving, (he was emotional as he left).

Mike was somewhat excited about the fact that they read his story. That they grieved, that they cared. This seemed to take on a significance importance in his recovery efforts.

*   *   *

I hadn't seen or heard from Mike for a few weeks I had sent emails but no response I figured he was sick but on the contrary he had not taken a drug for weeks and was feeling great. He invited me to an inside club pick-up tennis game because it had been raining for 5 days straight. He was using his free-court-pass. He couldn't wait another minute to play. He was more energetic than I had seen in months; happy, joking, the real Mike.

It was a good game (Mike was forgetful and a bit stiff), but overall he enjoyed the game as we switched partners each set. I was quite generous to him but didn't need to be. I wanted him to have a good week of tennis memories . . . He was heading for a mega chemo dose in two days. His final dose. The Doctors were surgically inserting a port in his chest that discharges the chemical 48 hours straight. '*Dog food!*'

It's a shame that his cure is what is hurting him the most.

I was surprised to see him drinking alcohol after the game, I didn't know what to make of it, but let it go.

I gave him the newspaper article from our tournament escapades. It told how we made it to the semifinals only to lose to the eventual winners. They didn't mention there were only four teams. He couldn't wait to show his son, and coworkers.

He says he is going on a super exercise regiment, to build up as much strength as possible. So he can function at a high level as long as possible.

A couple weeks later we met again. A beautiful night under the lights on the outside playground courts. Tennis was a salvation for him—he didn't have to think about tests results or time, he just played.

He's slow but in good spirits. He took off his hat, to wipe his brow and I could see his hair was nearly gone, white and thin and matted down from sweat. On the way out he had asked a couple guy's to share a pizza, his treat. Declining, they had dinner waiting for them at home. He didn't ask me, which I thought was odd but ok. As everyone scurried off, I stayed to make sure his car started etc . . . Something was different about him, unsettled. He informed me that he was going to have a huge test to determine his '**life expectancy**' in the morning. "Talk about a big test . . ." Is he well enough to continue treatment, or too far gone and released to live out his last days.

He called me as soon as he got the news—he had the best possible results! He is in remission!!! *No cancer cells detected*!

I can't wait to see him Monday at tennis. I wanted to bear-hug him. He didn't show up Monday but Lance his best friend did. I told Lance to call tonight and get the good news from him personally. They haven't talked all summer.

Last night I had a terrible nightmare.—It was of Mike and his illness, did he tell a fib? Maybe he didn't want everyone feeling sorry for him while he only had a shorten time to live. It would stop the stares and questions and maybe bring a few old friends back to him for the short time he had left. I want to confront him—let him know I will be around either way and can keep his secret.

He has not responded to my emails for at least two weeks. Finally a response, he assures me he is fine and back to work, slowly getting his life back together. Work takes all his energy right now but he is on the right track. His mind is starting to focus better, but he is holding off playing tennis for a while. He fought through the pain when he thought each moment could be his last. Now he was going to wait for his hands and feet to toughen up.

It all made sense . . . He was still working. The end of the summer followed with less and less contact. He doesn't return my emails, says he's been busy. None of my friends have seen him lately. It's been two months for me. He said he was off all medication for now and feeling much better.

He had wanted me to understand the huge impact of prayer. Thanked me for helping him get through his life crisis. Death is a perplexing thing. If you were in his place how would you handle it? I might not tell a soul. To look in those eyes.—

The countdown begins (*Christmas—2010'*)

It's been four months after Mike gave me the good news of the cancer being in remission. Very little contact from Mike only a few emails few and far between. Mostly good comments; work is good, but busy. A new Government missile project was starting perfect for his expertise. He seemed excited about that. (Needed)

He did reinforce the impact playing the tournament had on him while he was sick. "It gave him the Will to go on." He told me he was writing a story about his best friend (me) nursing him through another battle . . .

This one was really a life and death fight. I can't wait to read it. (*Never did see it.*)

I leave him alone except for a couple hello emails a week,—usually with no response. He isn't a big email fan.

A long packed email came today. In the long letter one sentence haunts me. He wrote;

"I'd like to hear more about your writing, I'm in a different state of mind these days. I realize my life expectancy is still around *12 months*; but I'm thinking more in terms of twenty years; and maybe

168

dying of something other than cancer. I believe we are all on a short time line. I hope we can be winning doubles championships in the far-out future in HEAVEN. Believe me there is a God who is very forgiving."

"Also, if it's possible *please add my name to the story we wrote.*"

My worst nightmare about Mike came true—I have to make sure but I believe he is telling me something I didn't want to hear. Has he stopped treatments and given up?

He assures me all is well, he just had a emotional moment.

Several weeks pass without a response when an urgent email from Mike arrives, I always have mixed emotions when his name appears on the computer. He wants to see me in person before he goes to the doctor for an update. Take a dog slog through the woods (a little slower than jogging with our pets). Or bring me to his church etc . . . I straight-out ask him if he's still on a 12 month schedule, because if he is I will be at his doorstep helping him get the most out of his last moments,—but if he is doing good then I have farm chores and Christmas (a Crazy Schedule) to contend with (being two weeks before Christmas). I will see him after the holidays.

What a *Dog Foodin' Dumb-ass disgusting* thing to write him! He had avoided me for the last few months I didn't feel so close to him at that moment. I had felt abandoned as he started to feel better. I was remorseful for being so blunt to put it lightly.

That weekend I finished my farm chores early and it was relatively warm outside. I called his house to ask if he wanted to bring his dogs to my farm and walk the woods. No answer, so I left a message.

He called back in tears stuttering, "I'll be there in 15 minutes." We walked and talked for hours as the dusk brought on the cold. Swapping sports stories until we froze. He can't wait for more days like these he insists, . . . "please lets do it again." It snowed that night. A fresh cleansing newborn feel. I expected a lot of negativity about my farm or my way of life instead he was the perfect friend. Life is good,—if only for a moment.

*   *   *

Mike called last night, to ask me to the Superbowl party. The one he didn't think he would attend this year.

Other news was the cancer is back in his throat and he was having tests to see just how much. I hear very little from him these days. I would love to join him at the party, but I am very shy in those situations, and Mike has a habit of showing a mean streak with me around. He tends to have to demean me in public. Maybe this would be different, but I can't take the chance of hurting our relationship at this point. I really want him to be with his friends. I will give him my time when I can get his full attention. As it turned out I was at the peak of a bad flu bout. It would be tough to make friends while coughing and sneezing.

I received an email from my (Harvard alumnae) friend Karen, expressing how charming Mike was at the party telling all of his adventures with me over the years. They had a mutual friend to talk about instead of concentrating on his illness. Mike calls me his renaissance man 'RM'. They had a great evening and I feel I was a part of it.

Flash forward a couple of month to Memorial Day—The first outside get together of the summer playground tennis.

No one has seen much of Mike, He had avoided everyone and concentrated on work.

He showed up late as usual but in good spirits.—The weather was perfect for tennis.

He played great, not very mobile but if it was near him,—he was unstoppable.

We played until we couldn't see anymore,—no lights tonight the town shut them down to save money.

We talked for at least an hour after everyone left until the mosquitoes were too overwhelming, just catching up. We discussed the bible—he was surprised I read it and was familiar with the entire book. He is off chemo because it isn't working anymore (bad sign,) but they are still trying other things and he is going for a big test this week.

I was in the truck ready to go home waiting for him to go first, in case he needed a hand. He walked over to me and said he had a tough question to ask.—Where would he go for a burial plot in this town?—wow—A sobering closing comment if I may say so myself.

The next week he is playing pretty good, he hasn't had the chemo for a while and his body is getting stronger.

He says, "I can tell you really care I can see it in your face. When I talk to you I feel a weight lifted off me." "Sometimes I just need someone to vent to—somebody that understands what I'm going through." He told me, now, that the end is in sight he feels like a millionaire. He doesn't have to worry about retirement.

As I try to rap my brain around these comments he invited me to New York for the US Open Tennis Extravaganza all expenses paid.

I have to go with him, I've never been and I know I could be the perfect road trip pal.

He was so excited he told everyone over the next week and invited several friends and was now hiring a bus the end of August. This will be the greatest memorial to him. Something that will be talked about for years. He called it his 'Swan Song.'

You have to admit it was pretty clever. Maybe Genius!

We haven't seen each other in three weeks. The playground courts have been rained out every Monday.

This week the weather is perfect and Mike can't wait to play. He even leaves work early to arrive on time. He knows next week will be a tough week with a large dose of a new experimental Chemo planned. He may not be up to playing for a while after this.

The good and bad news is he is back on treatments. It was made to act very aggressive on his particular cancer cells. They didn't use this before because of the harsher side effects. The safer chemo wasn't effective anymore. He had already had several smaller treatments with good results but it was really affecting his overall physical condition.

He jumps into play with extra gusto tonight extra trash talk—and an extra large smile.

Playing hard in the late sun has worn him thin and he had had his fill tonight. Satisfied with winning most of his games. He is exhausted but it is a good tiredness. He enjoyed every second he was out there. Toweling off and sipping the last of his Gatorade, every sip seemed to be more painful than the last.—This was a mild victory.

Two pretty girls arrive there late thinking the court lights would go on any minute. We knew the girls and watched as they warmed up while we talked. They called over to Mike and asked for a grudge match. (They didn't know he had been sick). Mike and I had played them last year, during a pretty rough time of chemotherapy and they almost beat us. Tonight was not a good time for a grudge match.—Mike was spent. He had not eaten yet because his throat was swollen and stomach had shrunk. So the now tasteless food was a task he forced himself to do out of necessity. He was on his way home to force some down now. The new experimental chemo was really affecting him, but a challenge like this was hard to pass up. So up and out on the court we go. Into battle mode. Not only did the girls trash-talk Mike, he also got a ribbing from the guys as they left as well. He basked in this.

Mike was full into the match but running on fumes. He was dehydrating as well. But he wasn't going to stop . . . He wasn't going to let cancer take this away from him. He had trouble recovering any energy at all, and went well beyond empty. Darkness came on quickly with the impending storm clouds overhead.

We finally won, but it didn't come soon enough. As we were gathering our gear to go home I didn't noticed Mike had walked across the parking lot and found a picnic table to lay on and passed out. Mike had dehydrated, when he came-to he was disorientated and dizzy for quite some time. Luckily I had a few energy snack bars in my truck, we each ate one sipping water as we sat and talked. He seemed to fully regain his constitution, but it was a long slow ride home as I followed him. He wouldn't let me drive him. The new drug was too lethal and he still had a larger dose planned for this week. This was bad, as it sucked the life out him.

His liver was failing. (This was his final match). He had contracted Hepatitis and lost almost fifty pounds in six weeks as his body shut down.

I am starting his job this week. Totally renovating his home mainly for selling, a complete outside makeover. Ordering the dumpster and the clapboards to get started. He had an MRI and found a blockage in his liver. They immediately prepped him for surgery to have it removed, hopefully it will help and bring him around. The surgery was a success but knocked him for a loop keeping him in the hospital. I was hoping to spend time with him while I was working at his home, but he was now in a rehab facility.

A week goes by and I get a disturbing email.—He wants to see me.

Come into the hospital and read him the story we wrote.—Hard not to get emotional. Mike quoted to me on the phone from his hospital bed, "I could have been a better person," "Yes I helped all I could, said my prayers, put money in the collection basket, Never swore, never used the lords name in vain, never strayed from my wife, etc . . . but I could have done more, should have done more."

How do you convince a dying man he had done enough to walk through the pearly gates of heaven? You did what you thought was right at that time.

He mentioned 'Job' the biblical character, the man that had everything including the respect of God.

Satan placed a bet with God saying if 'Job' wasn't so blessed he would denounce God. 'Job' lost everything; his family, his wealth, his health, but still believed God had a reason to put him through such pain. 'Job' eventually regained his health and made a new life for himself even better than before. Mike has the same plan. To stay with the Lord even if it means he must meet the maker himself. It's hard not to believe him. He signed off, (not by saying goodbye), but by saying he loves me, without hesitation I said "me too." He hung up with a little giggle.

To live like you are dying. I ponder if I would rather die in the flash of a camera,—or have an extra year to experience the seasons, and my loved ones. Would the pain and suffering be worth it? Would I find out I didn't have the friends I thought? Would they tire of me or bask in the few remaining moments and enjoy life more because of me?

Finally I was going to visit tonight; I had been warned of his looks. He had lost seventy pounds and was a shell of his former self. I expected the worst as I waited to go in a little late so I wouldn't bother any other guests. I walked past his door, hearing his voice I stepped back and peeked into the door and saw an old man.

He was sitting up tall in his chair, thin face, glowing yellow. His hair buzz-trimmed tight to his head. It only took me a few minutes to get past the looks and enjoy the visit. His son was there probably happy to have some comic relief, (he had been coming every night). He was really easy to talk with as well.

I had commented that it must have been tough to be the son of such a good athlete, with so much competitive instincts. Junior smiled and told me on the contrary as a child he thought he was the best athlete in the world because he never lost. Until he was 10 years old when Dad decided to (throw-down) and teach him to be humble. Mike Jr. couldn't believe how incredible his father was or how he could get so good overnight. It was a good story and I could see a strong bond between them. Mike's face lit up as Junior reminisced.

After our initial hellos and meeting his son in the hospital room Mike asked me to tell his son how devoted I was to helping my grandmother.

Of course I relished the thought of remembering granny (she had just passed this week (100 yrs old). "Oh ya" I started, Every Saturday we would meet for homemade pizza and every Wednesday night I brought her to visit a relative, then that progressed to a movie once a week. Etc . . . until etc . . . Mike was always impressed with my granny stories, but I figured it was more calculating, . . . he wanted his son's devotion. I was his example.

The first time I saw junior's humor was a moment after this story as we sat in silence. Mike Sr. declared us both his #1 and #2 friends—I was at odds about the title (I couldn't be that high on his list.)

Both Jr. and I looked at each other and I suggested Jr. must be number #1. "Congratulations Junior."

He blurted out that after that granny story I was way ahead in the #1 voting as we both belly laughed.

I stated I was just glad to be on the list. Mike Sr. was a little put out with us carrying on at his expense.

Mike was happy to hear I had a video of us playing tennis in the championships. He wanted his son to see him play. I was just hoping to give him the drive to get better. He loved the videos, we watched them several hundred times. Either doing a running commentary or shutting his eyes and just listening.—He love the sound of the ball, the chatter, or even the birds in the background. He said he felt like he was really there, making me back it up to highlight any particular great moment. Luckily we won every run through, we won that championship over and over . . .

I'm looking forward to seeing him again. He's going to teach me how to play cribbage.

Mike mumbled during a slow march down the hall, dragging the feeding tube stand, "Family is what it all boils down to in the end. Family is all that matters . . . Out of every possible scenario,—it is family." "When I first heard of my plight, I went to the front office and asked for a suicide mission." If he was going to perish he wanted to go out in glory, with a huge wad of cash to help his loved ones. He was serious. He worked at a high level of government affairs. (Luckily there were no secret missions available.)

I visited several times in the next few weeks staying until midnight. I couldn't leave him. He wanted to stay awake as long as possible. To enjoy life and hoping that when he does sleep it will be sound and through til morning. There were several things that woke him—nurses and yelling patients were high on his list.

Mike was forced out of the hospital, (insurance was blamed). but he was well enough to come home and the doctors signed him out. He didn't want to leave,—he didn't want to be locked upstairs in a room they prepared for him—to die alone. He didn't want to be a burden to his wife.

I worked at his house through this time removing all the old siding and installing cedar clapboards. Repairing the severely rotted walls and trim. Then painting the entire house for resale. Nearly two months as the days got shorter and colder. At first we took several walks around his property a day, discussing his recovery. (He told me I could charge, 'time and a half' for the psychiatry work). I saw him a lot during this time, but slowly he stopped asking me in. I did get at least a smile and a wave everyday. Not feeling up to entertaining was his excuse. He barely watches TV—he just stared at it. He looks well, but I'm sure he is not doing well at all. He had just finished radiation treatments to open his throat to swallow.—If it works he will be put back on Chemo—the cancer hasn't been addressed in months. He is discouraged contemplating the long journey back to normalcy, and dreads going back on the aggressive chemo.

I will be going over next week to do some inside finish carpentry.—I hope he talks to me then. I begged a few friends to send cards, photos and prayers or call; to push him out of his depression. They responded valiantly glad to help in any way.

His feeding tube isn't working so well,—he is still losing weight. He needs to exercise but does not have the will. He told me he was giving up, "Please don't think less of me."

Again I am faced with the 'Ultimate Quandary.' If you had a choice would you choose to live for a year knowing you were dying? Time to contemplate the wonders of the universe, being able to experience one more Christmas winter, one more spring cleaning, sweat out one more summer on the courts and beach blanket. Say goodbye to your friends and loved ones, One more Superbowl. Get your affairs in order. Make amends with the lord, . . . and anyone you may have offended. Write a few memoirs. Search out the latest cures. Attend one more wedding to see all the relatives. Four seasons to walk the woods with the goldies. Pick your final resting place.

You will find out who your real friends are. You will be brought to the brink of caring, to the threshold of pain and suffering. Questioning the Lord as you beg to be with him. If I had a choice?

Laid to rest, never fit so perfectly.—"Rest in Peace my friend."

Michael died Christmas morning. Someone suggested, He was a present to God.

Mike's funeral was the hardest I've ever attended. I wanted to run and hide until it was over. I broke down at the slightest memory. I know he wanted me to read a passage from our story, and I rehearsed it many times over the past year. Never getting through the first paragraph. Mike's son read it for me. He had the bravery of his father. I saw it by the way he stood in front of all his relatives and his fathers friends and held it together long enough for us all to be with him one more time. Mike's son reminded me of myself . . . We would strive for Mike's respect only to find out we had been on the top of his **respect** list all the time. I was the butt of his jokes, (the fall guy)—not because he wanted to single me out and hurt me. It was because we were that close that he knew whatever he said would be understood as just plain brotherly teasing.

My condolence to Mike's wife Paula, enduring such a heartache.

My thoughts to Mike Junior; to experience 'Captain America' deteriorating before your eyes. To be helpless to save him. Dad was prouder of you than you could ever have imagined.

Mike was not afraid of dying, he just wanted to live forever.

Karen and Tom

Super Dave

Brothers in Arms

Richie   Do Bears sit in the woods?

The Hole

The Truth,—Simply 'Is'

When all the widows of the spirit have been nailed shut.
Do a big ol' canon ball right in the middle of it.
I did a "jackknife"

(Roger - 'American Dad')

The Naked Truth—Plain and unadorned

Truth and falsehood went skinny-dipping. Falsehood came out first dressed in truths clothing and departed. Truth not wanting to don the garments of falsehood, remained naked.

(Ancient Roman fable)

ξξ 'Coming of age' ξξ

"I was a Tennis instructor, in Hog-Eye, Missouri"
"Rock n' Roll Coulda-been"
In the eye of the beholder

The Truth,—Simply 'Is'

As a budding Blues guitarist, not just technically, but emotionally I was ripening, and blooming. I had the fire to make a guitar bitch and moan or scream bloody murder.

Graduating high school I had played a few years in local Boston bands, exciting, but a financial dead end track for sure. I decided I needed to take the next step if I wanted to make music a career, so I enlisted a local alumnus of the Berkeley College of Music to study 'music theory.' This was my sure fire way to be accepted into Berkeley. Finally, I was on the fast track, not waiting for a lucky break or other musicians/agents to dictate my future.

Halfway through my private studies I received a phone call from a distant cousin, this guy I hadn't seen for years. As teenagers he and his brothers had visited a few times from the Midwest. We shared a love of art and music, keeping in contact through the years sending tapes, photos and updates.

My cousins had gone on themselves to form a band, and had successfully landed a national US tour. The music scene at this time was starved for new talent. Punk rock was in its infancy, and this was the time to strike. This was our shot at the brass ring.

This call was an invitation to join them in Kansas City to start a seven-month road tour. Should I leave my college prospects, and family to join a working, paying, national caliber band?

A 'NO-BRAINER,' I mainly wanted to go to college to be in a position to get these opportunities. So I put college on hold, kissed my soul-mate goodbye and boarded a 747 to stardom. The possibility to play with: Santana, Kansas, Boston, ZZ Top, Rick Derringer, Gary Wright, Styx, Cheap Trick and possibly *KISS*, a young carnival band, with face paint, fire breathing pyrotechnics and blood showers. Now I'm really getting interested. We were slated to open for all these acts and more. Trekking across America during the next seven months. A dream come true. Scheduled to play in a new city every few weeks and between performances, we'd play smaller venues: bars, theaters, and small arenas, advertising the upcoming primary Concert.

The day I flew into Kansas City, I was shuffled into the penthouse offices of Chris Fritz, the biggest promoter in the Midwest. There, I was introduced to Carlos Santana and was invited to jam with him at the sound check that very night. A set up, 'of the good kind.' I admired his playing, and had thoroughly studied and performed his music for years. They knew I was a fan.

I played with Carlos not knowing if I should play his licks or something new. I did both. Playing through his amp standing next to him was heaven, and I was dancing on clouds. That night I was allowed to watch his performance from the wings. This was the perfect initiation to kick off my first road tour.

The second night, my cousin and I were back stage again. There to watch and get the feel of the rock star atmosphere, while checking out the hottest new band to emerge from the depth of Kansas City,—'Grand Max.'

We were slated to perform with them later in the summer. They were the main attraction, the headline act with a '3-D Laser Light show' promoted as the opening act. That's right, just a light show. The newest futuristic happening back then (before disco). The light show went on as planned but the band was nowhere in sight. Word had it they were on route, but the buzz backstage was chaos . . . My cousin, (a bass player) jokingly suggests he and I take the stage with the roadie drum technician. Heck, we could jam.

He suddenly turned serious,—this was a brave undertaking.—"Come on! We don't even have to sing, just rock-out." . . . I was game, after I threw up . . . We had not played together yet, and I had never played in front of this many people before.

The light show had gone over its allowed time, and the crowd was getting restless. As impressive as it was, like a fireworks display going on too long, you become bored and stop looking up anticipating the grand finale. The audience started to boo and chant for the main act.

The Drum tech jumped on the kit and started a drum solo with the laser lights still blazing on the curtain behind him. The crowd cheered, but really, how long can a drum solo last? We found out that night, (not long.) I grabbed the guitar leaning against the amp and plugged in. Creating a thunderous ear-splitting feedback whistle that wouldn't stop even as I moved away from the amp. Panicking, I figured out that I could control the feedback with the position of the guitar and volume knob. I started to shake the neck wildly as it sputtered and farted. The crowd was on their feet in awe wanting to be entertained. I grabbed the whammy bar and vibrated it to death. I made like it was all on purpose. With the drums pounding savagely behind me, the soundboard engineer adjusted the main controls, and the real guitar sound took over. I gyrated, and posed as I spewed battalions of notes keeping up with the drummer. I started playing a primitive riff that I'd been working on at home, heavy almost tribal, mesmerizing, as the drummer settled into a throbbing cadence. The crowd was being seduced. Before they could grasp the situation my shirtless cousin ran out from behind the wall of amplifiers playing a rumbling low bass note that blended perfectly with my riffs.

We were Rock Gods! Static electricity shot through my spine as I started to improvise (this was my specialty). I must have played every lick, every Blues/Rock scale front and backwards, every lead guitar cliché I knew, from all the best guitarist (Clapton to Hendrix.) . . .

This was the Song of Songs . . . The drummer led us through a gamut of changes, and syncopations, and we followed, changing patterns as the last wore thin. When he slowed the pace I started to play classical scales, they fit like a glove, but my favorite and oddest matches were the flamingo clichés into Egyptian sounding patterns. My Mentor would have been proud to see all the hard work we had done being put to use.

This was invigorating; the importance of the moment had pushed us all into a blending of minds transfixed in time. We took the audience with us as they stood hypnotized spellbound staring, mouths open. This was better than any drug. Pure kinetic energy, channeling the swarm into 'one' free entity. Three thousand spirits blending together focused on a single tick.

At one point as the music crescendoed into a frenzy, the bass player jumped up on a stage monitor. Motioning me over he leapt onto my shoulders. Luckily, I was an ex-footballer and he was a featherweight. This was uncomfortable for me, but it was pure genius. It was hard to keep my balance with him rocking viciously, choking me with his legs and thumping my head with his guitar. The drummer quieted down and I stopped playing, as my cousin started a bass solo.

Worse yet, he would hock up a louie and spit straight up in the air and try to catch it in his mouth, (not being very successful), each time raising a rowdy Bronx cheer. I bent forward and slid him off my neck, and without skipping a beat he flew to the tip of the stage and spewed out the biggest chunk of disgusting phlegm maybe twenty feet into the audience and abruptly stopped playing. Dead silence. Almost like it was choreographed, the clustered masses seemed to take in a deep breath and on cue, spouted back. Like the discharge from a blowhole, a glorious site to behold. Of course, none of the spittle could reach us, but there were a lot of damp heads in the first few rows. We went on with the jam for a short time as I was inevitably being waved off the stage. The real band was there, and our job was done.

We had saved the day . . . The applause was deafening, exhilarating, still ringing in my ears as I laid awake in bed with no one to share this perfect moment with. Ok maybe it was over stating the situation, but this was our time, and we seized the day.

This I tell because the buzz we created earned us a few better spots on our upcoming tour. Like Arrowhead football stadium in Kansas City with Peter Frampton and Steve Miller in front of 60 thousand screaming fanatics.

We literally were 'Rock Stars'.

Nothing could stop us now

My cool cousin arranged this whole tour by dating the receptionist of the biggest tour manager in the Midwest. Impressing the big-wigs enough to sign his band to the tour, 'a real fast talker.' That's when they called me, I had the flash and *stage presence*. A big muscular guy with big hair and a knack for screaming solos. We would be the 'Opening Act,' the warm up, no pressure, just get the crowd jumping! The grosser the better, punk was in it infancy. This was going great!

Before I joined them, they were a mere southern rock bar band . . . My cousin had told me he was never so free to be himself on stage until he played with me. I brought the needed, flare, originality, and theatrics, Alice Cooper-esque performances. Not to toot my own horn, but I loved to play the part; in the mirror, or front and center stage. It was a game I took pleasure in, I basked in it.—I was a thespian of Rock.

Until;

It all went to my psychotic, cousin's head, a young handsome, raging hormonal bass player and now, 'Punk Rock Star.'

Halfway through the tour he suddenly went over the deep end.

He just snapped.

I portrayed *the part of a Rock Star,* **He lived it**.

Spending money like a millionaire Rapper, writing checks; fancy restaurants, and new equipment, exotic guitars, hair stylists, drugs, drinks and expensive wardrobe . . .

"*He did it all for the Band,*" he would say. He used all the groups' petty cash, then our living expense funds, used it all and kept writing checks . . . It's funny with all the excess going on he was only nailed for a bounced check . . . ok, but several thousands worth. (Bank fraud.)

The local small town court Judge, his Hicksville lawyer and *parents,* agreed on a settlement for the bank fraud. Demanding he have a steady job back home where he had to work full time (at the 3M tape factory), with his wages garnished straight to the Bank, (Missouri's court system worked pretty harsh on delinquent hippies).—They didn't hear the part, where he could pay this off

185

with petty cash, at the end of the tour when we got paid, if we were to continue the tour. No, they wanted this punishment to stick to his ribs. A lesson for all us long haired juveniles.

Maybe his parents had much more to do with it. (?)

We still had the big arena gigs to make the best of a shitty situation, with a whole lot of free time in between.

'The Back of Beyond'
Life in the rolling hills of a backwoods Midwestern town:

Threatened, by corporate lawyers to be removed from the tour and sued for breach of contract, we settled for a time out. All small gigs were canceled, but we salvaged the big important shows . . . Now having to stay in Shitscreek, Missouri during the week (the band's family home-base). I had to find entertainment. Way too much time on my hands.

There were only a few jobs, available in a small town in the Midwest within walking distance . . . Smelting, cleaning bed pans at the loony bin and coal mining were not high on my list!

To keep in shape I started exercising at the local youth center and boxing with the local police and teens. Ultimately they asked if I would help run a basketball and tennis camp. This was right up my alley.

Tennis I didn't know much about back then, but I thought I did. Hell, I knew a lot more than they did. I knew some rules and I was good at patty-cake tennis. I knew games and drills to play (that my brother and I did as a kid). I even taught my younger cousin to play so he could impress his high school sweet heart.

We all played for hours on the courts behind the Abbey run—Cottey College; I remember winning many Mr. Pibb sodas, their price for losing, garnering me the nickname Mr. Pibb. I drank it by the pail-full. It was cheap and on-tap at the local Mom-and-Pop store across the street from the courts. I had never heard of it until I landed here. It had the taste of victory, with a little cherry flavoring.

Even though I was an athlete, not a tennis player, I was the best player in the whole town, and took on all comers. Then we'd head over to the gym to shoot hoops or box, sparring with the biggest softest gloves, so no one really got hurt, but you knew when a good punch landed.

I was the Michael Jordan of Shitscreek, the shorter, hairier, penniless white version. Alright, how about a cross between a young Rocky Balboa and a hairy Rambo. The first Rocky movie had recently come out, which made boxing en-vogue.

Tennis was a huge part of keeping my sanity taking up a bunch of my time, but it didn't pay much. My stashed cash was running low and I needed spending money fast.

Soon I was talked into working for the railroad.

A flier in the store window caught my attention; Ten miles of tracks were being laid to attach a new farm supply business.

I've been workin' on the railroad.

It wasn't so hard to talk me into it, they said I wouldn't last a day pounding railroad spikes. A nickel a spike. This I had to try. How tough could it be? I was in the best shape of my young life.

I made a whopping ten bucks cash my first day. The water, sunburn and blisters were all free.

In the process, I met an old Indian, a frail old coot. He said he was from the Osaga Indian tribe. I thought he was mentally handicap at first then I figured he was the town drunk. He worked the handcar pump trolley, our only means of transportation to the job site, it had arms that pivoted seesaw-like on a base, that you pull up and push down to make the cart travel over the rails.

He would drop us off and make several trips for supplies and water . . . So brittle a man you could see his skeletal outline. His skin charred, steely with deep-pitted wrinkles. He would go into a trance pedaling the cart for miles without a drop of sweat. I found out later he really wasn't that old but back then thirty was over the hill.

It would take him a while to break his trance-like state, in order to be talked to. I offered him half my sandwich one day, he wouldn't take it. He needed to fast, in order to go into his trance state, *"no food,"* he would bark. I started to bring him a sandwich of his own each day and told him to take it home with him, if he didn't want it now. He warmed up to me, and we seemed to become friends or at least he wasn't afraid of me, and in the process, I got the other workers to be nicer to him.

He saw I had bad blisters from swinging the oversized spiking maul all day and gave me an odd salve that dried them up and made my hands numb almost instantly. I never bothered to ask what it was, just from the smell of it, not really wanting to know. It made your skin rough and awkward to bend (not so good for guitar playing). He also gave me tips on meditating while I pounded spikes, getting me into a rhythm, to a good mental place where you didn't fight the hammer you *became the hammer*. It came easy to me I even stopped overtly sweating, in fact, I stopped eating and began to fast all day myself. Not on purpose I just wasn't hungry. Water was hardly needed, even my asthma didn't bother me while on these workdays. I began to look forward to being in the trance-state it made me strong and invincible and calm, at-one with the world.

The head honcho offered me triple wages to encourage me to return. I became the best spiker in town history (?) soon to be a hundredaire. Move over John Henry a new folklore was taking over. Being paid in cash each day gave you such feeling of accomplishment.

Interlude:

I longed to be in the trance as it became an obsession. Looking back, I was depressed and homesick, this being the first time away from my mom and leaving my girlfriend, my high school sweetheart, my soul-mate behind. Not to mention the tour being dissected keeping only the bigger arena gigs.

I had seen a lot of pain and devastation emerge from alcohol and drugs, affecting friends, family and celebrities. I was determined to avoid that unbeatable fate. I was a health nut from years of sports, totally against drugs and alcohol. Drugs, didn't agree with me as well, the few times I was tempted . . . I needed all my faculties to survive and push my music career which I was totally serious about. So I believe I turned to the meditation stuff just to survive. Elvis had just died this week, of a drug overdose. If the king couldn't handle them what chance would I have?

Now the good stuff:

I decided one night to use my trance state while I went for my ritual midnight run to the only payphone in town, a mile away, where I would call my sweetheart (collect) each night.

That night I skipped dinner still fasting from the days work and put the rhythm of my footsteps to a 'chant' Injun Jo had been humming that day. It was an odd rhythm that had off beats at different intervals a bit hard to learn I recall, but it made you concentrate at a super high level. I was light on my feet that night, so much that I couldn't feel the road. I realized I couldn't hear my footsteps. In fact, I was seeing myself from the back,—from an odd angle,—from above. I wasn't shocked, it felt normal as I rose upward.

I was flying above myself, like I was a kite, being pulled along by a string. Looking down, my body appeared strong with long shoulder length curly dark hair flowing with each stride. I was not a good long distant runner; I was big and muscular, better suited to run a steeplechase, thick powerful legs and big ass, far from being a marathon runner. I had asthma and hated even to jog. Normally, I fought every step and labored begrudgingly. I always enjoyed the stopping part, feeling proud of myself, but I never felt that runners high.

This was a real runners high now. I was moving at a sprinters pace effortlessly but not headed for town I DIDN'T WANT ANY DISTRACTIONS I wanted to run—to fly.

After a while, I (my consciousness) broke the umbilical cord and flew off and up. I went towards the lights in the town center. Nothing was happening there, a ghost town at this hour, but something was drawing me here.

I didn't feel the desire, to do flips or dive-bombs, I just moved from place to place . . . Seeing the phone booth reminded me I was supposed to make a call, I was really late, would she still be waiting. I went by the phone booth but realized I couldn't dial. Panicking I starting to sob as I found myself back in my body running, flowing, smooth at a nice even clip,—weeping. In time my asthma caught up to me, and I started to wheeze. Losing focus, the pace slowed to a trudge. I hadn't sweated a drop, (possibly because I didn't drink anything that day) and was terribly dehydrated. I actually didn't know where I was.

I bet I was 15 miles out in East Bumfutch, and very thirsty, and *hungry*, and dizzy.

I agonized, "It will take me all night to walk back." It was a gravel road, and there was no traffic or houses. I headed back at a crisp walking pace for a good hour. Feeling unsettled I had to take a break, so I sat down at the side of the road and leaned against an old willow. The full moon lit up the area giving off odd shadows, causing shapes to bend and sway. I remember staring at the moon thinking this is probably something I shouldn't be doing. Going over what had just happened tonight, the feeling of speed and weightlessness and the never ending energy of 'flight.' I passed out.

I awoke to an old man motioning at me to get in the back of his unearthly, loud farm truck. "I guess they don't need mufflers out here." He dropped me off at my doorstep, without a word spoken. He must have known me; I swear I heard him say my name, as he drove off. He looked so familiar, I felt I knew him, but couldn't quite make out his face, it all seemed blurred. I wandered into an empty house, slurped down a bowl of cereal and went upstairs to bed. Slept straight through the day, then through the night and awoke fresh ready for work the next day. (I missed a whole day). The odd thing was nobody tried to wake me or even noticed. The family never mentioned it. I got up and eagerly headed for work only to find no one at the train track junction where Injun Jo picked us up.

Of course, *it was Saturday* . . . As I started for home I heard the cart rattling down the track, it was Jo.

As he pulled up to the loading dock I told him I was surprised to see him on a Saturday, he said he was there just for me, he knew I would be there. I just let that go. I thought I heard him wrong in his broken muttered English. He accepted my offer to buy him breakfast around the corner at the streetcar diner. The place was empty, "odd for a Saturday."

We went in, and I proceeded to tell him about flying. He was very upset even scared for me, warning me not to use a trance, this way. I could have been killed or worse. He went on and on about the dangers of not reattaching, something about some friends in the loony bin.

This is where he offered to show me a safe journey into a spiritual plane of existence . . . No drugs involved but fasting (*no food*) was required. That ended my breakfast plans. Jo ate both plates of eggs and grits, "I think I see a little meat on his bones" as I poke his ribs in jest.

I don't remember having a decent meal in days, oddly enough I wasn't hungry. I decided to checkout the towns annual 'Hog-Eye Day' Bar-B-Q, just across the street. That's where everyone was. I just followed the parade outside of the diner. I had forgotten there was a town get-together today. That's what Jo was in town for.

Stepping out of the diner I was swept up into the proceedings and became part of the parade waving and mocking the kids, as they teased back, "It's Mr. Pibb." It was more of a cattle-drive than a parade. Marching band, drum and fife, possum pie, cotton candy, popcorn, baked goods, fried everything and open pit barbecuing. All free and the foods and smells were engulfing me. It smelt great but, I wasn't hungry. I just walked around in a daze.

That night I met Jo around midnight at the track junction, (I'm sorry to have to call him Injun Jo, but it fits). I jumped on the seesaw cart, and off we went. I noticed that he didn't seem so distant, (Maybe because he was eating better). He stopped a few miles out, and we pulled the cart off the tracks. This, I found out later was his home, an old abandoned shack more like an outhouse. From the smell, it could have been. We went into the field and laid in the fresh cut hay, He just stared at me. I'd understood very little about this phenomenon, and I wanted to know more. What was going on here? What was this serene spirit state that will give me all the answers? I had to know more. Was this known to many, why didn't everyone know this? Could I meet Elvis's recently deceased spirit?

He told me not just anyone could do this? In my mind the fasting seemed to be the key (hallucination). I thought to myself, "Michael you've been in Missouri too long. Get out now before it's too late. Look what it's done for him". OK, maybe that's what I would think now, but back then it was something new and exciting. It was my drug at the moment. Anyway, self-doubt was nothing new to me.

Something was calling "Me," I had opened myself up to the spirit world and it was pulling me in, and Jo was my guide, whether he liked it or not.

"Old Jo," (Maybe that's a better name for him even though he's wasn't old) suggested I try 'spiritual travel.'

I don't remember what he called actually it, I believe it was an old Indian name, if he really was an Indian.

"This is *not* an out-of-body experience, this was much safer," he assured me, "an inner body cleansing."

As I lay motionless he just stared at me. For the first time in days I was thinking of how hungry I was and wondering how much longer this was going to be. How good those eggs would be right now. That odd smell was making me hungry, and a little bit nauseous.

He spoke in tongues, (that sounds more interesting than; he mumbled inaudibly). He started a small campfire, he said to scare off the wolves and bears. Huh? I recalled staring into the flame as it danced. Its fingers were reaching out to me. I focused hard on one particular kindle arc.

In my mind, I heard his voice clear as day, *"Picture a light from the top of your head.".* It wasn't just words, but flashing images . . . spinning white spirals . . . *"Imagine yourself going through it moving up to a spiritual plane."* This was what I heard, who knows what Jo actually said. In fact, as I meditate on this, the voice was very familiar. A voice from my past, soothing, reassuring, Safe.

The place appeared to me as an iridescent cloud of smoldering haze.

So far, so good. I now see why people so often imagined heaven as a misty cloudy place. A very agreeable nebular, peaceful. Now I'm floating amongst the golden mist.

I felt fine,—at peace.

Jo asks in a clear easy voice, *"Do you see anything?"*

I didn't as I looked full circle. "No."

"Stay still,"

Then I saw a blurred human outline, I couldn't make it out but I grasped whom it was.

My girlfriend's father, 'Aubrey.' He had died about a year prior, His death was extremely traumatic to me, watching the pain of love-ones left behind. I was in the midst of a family holocaust. I had never experienced death so close, funerals, wakes, and gravesites and total life changes. He had always frightened me, being my girlfriend's father and all.

He gestured to me, and I nodded back. I was surprised to see him, but I had no particular need to speak to him, in fact, I felt a kind of respect radiating from him an acceptance, as he moved on. I waited in silence.

As a child I'd spend entire afternoons in the pool, holding my breath and floating underwater, calm, silent and free. No up or down,—no sound, no gravity no worries just nothingness. It drew me. Two minute slices of self-possession. This is what was racing through my head.

Jo, invades the tranquility, *"What's happening?"* It echoes and fades to stillness.

"Nothing," for what seemed like forever.

A slight glow, a spark of light gradually swelling. "Its, its,—my father." I revealed somewhat shocked. I sensed him before he fully materialized.

I became anxious.

I hadn't had an easy time with my father. Teenage angst, rebellion stuff. We bumped heads occasionally. I had mentally abandoned him. He didn't understand me as an Artist/ Musician –that's not good in the old traditional Italian ways he was raised. You can't make a living from that.

He had died suddenly from a heart attack at the young age of 48 just a few months after my girlfriend's father died. He wasn't even sick, I remember leaving work, rushing my mother to the hospital, only to meet the doctor in the hallway shaking his head (no), saying, "I'm sorry," as my mother collapsed to the floor. I didn't understand, "you're sorry about what?" How did you know why we were here?

Death wasn't even a possibility. I went total numb, for days on end. Two traumatic life-altering ordeals so close together. Fathers don't die.

He would never have approved of this spiritual mumbo jumbo. Or playing rock n' roll. Or pretty much anything I did. We hadn't talked seriously in years before he passed.

I did once feel his ghost-hand on my shoulder while I was speeding toward a green-lighted intersection, in the old Chevy van I inherited from him. I immediately slowed down as a car flew past me followed by high-speed police cruisers. My loud radio had blocked the sirens—a sure crash at high speed avoided. I knew it was him, I can still feel his hand on my shoulder. That impression never left me.

Now he was showing up while I was vulnerable, in an altered state of consciousness.

Drawing closer he looked the same, No, he looked much younger the way I remembered him best, stocky without the thinning graying hair. He was translucent and misty, like everything else around him. I wanted to tell him I loved him. I wanted him to be proud of me. I was on edge.

Without warning, he took me in his arms.

In the instant of embrace, I saw and felt everything in my relationship with my father, all the feelings he had had and why he had found me so difficult, all the feelings I had had and why I had misunderstood him, all the love that there was between us, and all the confusion and misunderstandings that over powered it. I had seen all the things he had done for me and all the ways he had helped me. I saw every aspect of our relationship at once, the way you can take a glance at a familiar face and immediately recognize that person. It was an instant of compassion, acceptance and love.

I burst into tears.

And it was done,—over—completed.

What I meant was that this incredibly powerful experience had already happened, complete and total, in a fraction of a second. The moment I burst into tears it was finished, he was gone, we never said a word. There was no need to speak.

I opened my eyes and I sprang right out of the trance-state and stood up, and said,

"Let's eat, I'm starving." I couldn't explain it to myself, I couldn't really explain it to anyone. It was more of a feeling of satisfaction, contentment, of well being, and now . . . hunger.

I was in awe at the speed it had happened. Something profound had occurred and was resolved in a wink of an eye. This gave me a new perspective on life. Old dogmas were cast aside, shackles shattered. There was an exhilarating sense of freedom lifting my inner being. . . . It had a truly cathartic cleansing effect on me.

I worked with Jo just a few weeks after this, but we never tried the spiritual witch doctor stuff again. Somehow this experience took away my desire to go further into the spirit world, and soon I lost interest altogether.

Thinking back I can deduce, and hypothesize.

It was as if someone was calling me to this experience, and now it isn't necessary. I don't know why I didn't pursue it more. Jo even seemed to know it was over. Something in my head just put it all aside, almost forgotten, like a dream, you remember it, but it just fades into the background. I got what I wanted, and the need wasn't there anymore. Of course I tried it again but never made it past '*hungry.*'

I did jog late at night several more times in a trance, a runner's trance. Funny I could never remember that Indian chant. Jo would tell me it, when I asked him, but it never seemed to be the same one. Jo could have been the medium my dad used to bring me to him. Jo was always in a trance an easy target for the spirit world.

I did later learn that this town had one of the biggest insane asylums, Mental State Hospital number 3, and it was nick named "Lunatic Asylum" by the State. This is where my cousin's father worked twenty years as a Minister. Jo may have been a walk-in? I had turned down an offer to work there, I had nightmares thinking of the odd jobs they would have asked me to do.

Hog-Eye was the original name of the town, and was still revered and celebrated. Changed, over a hundred years ago to Nevada, MO.

I don't know who the truck driver was, never saw him again. No one recognized my description. I don't really know where I was that night or how sick I was, or if I could have made it back on my own. I have no idea how far I had been. I even drove down several roads looking for the one I was on.

At the conclusion of the tour, I was invited to relocate to California to regroup, with a slight roster change and start all over again, minus the hay fields. As tempting as that was, I didn't enjoy a single part of touring, except being on stage. I now believe, without the diversion of the outback, I would surly have succumbed to the vices of the business, because my adolescent mind was at a very vulnerable state. Alcohol and drugs were the only escape for this existence, cheap and easy access.

The crowning moment of the tour was the sixty thousand fans at Arrowhead stadium, (the sheer human volume). I'll never forget the audience erecting naked human pyramids, right in front of the stage. Not wanting to be upstaged, Peter Frampton wouldn't allowing us to have any special effects during our 30 minute stage show—no smoke, or fireworks, talk-boxes, or strobe lights. Just us 'Raw' and it was amazing. I did stop and stare at the 50 foot Video monitor across the stadium during my close-up. This was only topped by a spiritual visit from my Dad.

I came home without a doubt in my mind of what I wanted out of life and married my high school sweetheart, with the full consent of her late Dad. We didn't talk much about the tour because she was traumatized believing I would not ever want to come back home. She had good reason, I had always dreamt of being on the stage. Beware of what you wish for, it may not be worth the price. Suppressing these memories for more than thirty years I became very content to live my life in a small town in New England, as a carpenter (like my father) playing sports and music in local clubs and bars as a hobby.

I'm still happily married, until she reads this.

This miracle revelation was found in an old trunk stashed in the back of my subconscious like the old Thanksgiving-Day MVP football-trophy my friend Tom found 30 years later while I helped him clean out his attic. Out of sight out of mind. When he held that bronze football in his hands the images were as clear as the day he won it. I felt that same spark.

(In conclusion)

I believe it was an **enlightened hardcore Zen Buddhist Master** that once said;

Truth doesn't screw around, and truth doesn't care about your opinions, it doesn't care if you believe it. Oh, and one other thing: The truth is not open to negotiations—not by you, not by me, not by the moral majority. The **truth, simply Is.**

You eat truth, and excrete truth four hours later. Take a whiff—what a lovely fragrance the truth has. Then, you are hungry for more. (That part might have been Confucius).

This started out :
"I was once a Tennis instructor in Hog-Eye," and ended, "A True Love Story." I can't wait to tell you more about the rest of the tour.

'The End'

Fade to black—Cut! That's a wrap . . .
Roll Credits . . .

This is an interview with the author about this last story.

Left on the cutting room floor. Random thoughts and explanations
'This did not make the story'—probably for the better.
I hereby apologize to my cousins for any character depravations, or
mislaid embellishments.—Heck it happened over thirty years ago.

*Sitting out by the pool sipping coffee coolatta's the interviewer
asks: "Mike, I hate when books end right when they start to get
interesting, was there anything more you could tell us about Injun
Jo. I am fascinated with this story, tell us more. Please let us ease out
of this final story with a few explanations."

Injun Jo—had a bad habit of passing gas. All the time. I know
it's not that odd. However, he didn't realize how disrespectful that
was. He would lift a cheek and rip a loud one while he was talking
to you not skipping a beat. Except maybe to make a side comment
to himself if it had a rather robust odor, somewhat proudly. This
was as normal as coughing or sneezing for him. Not so great, in the
breakfast diner. The louder the better. It wasn't enough he didn't
bath regular and always had the same clothes everyday.

He was in his Sunday best on Hog day. I didn't notice until I saw
him riding that Bull.

The smell at the shack was a combo of manure and animal
carcasses. Wild animals would come to his place to die, usually
staying with him for up to a week before passing, only coming
within talking distance. He would talk to them, feed them and bury
them. He also collected animals that were killed in the road and bury
them. Not always having the energy to do it immediately he would

put them in plastic bags and hoist them in trees. Another smell was the hoards of left over food, (from the festivities) he was given for the animals.

Hog-Eye Day was Jo's favorite day of the year he was the honorary master of ceremonies. Every year riding the biggest oldest Texas Longhorn (his Beast of Burden) bringing up the rear of the parade. Commencing the start of the festivities and bringing luck to the town with his own interpretation of an Indian peace dance. Thanking the spirits for a good summer. We all called it his 'Happy Dance.' This was not done in jest.

As far as I know he was not a drunk, once proclaiming, "firewater was the downfall of humanity."

He had told me my aura (great spirit/chi) was very strong and bright, especially from the chest, heart area. With an exceptional halo glow from my head. He said that is what drew him to me. I thought it was the sandwiches.

Each night that I made the jog to the town square, this mangy dog would slip out from behind a tree. Not a particularly big dog. Along this quiet stretch of dense woods.

At first he would bark a warning as I passed, (a sort of keep away yip). Then as it became a ritual, he would be waiting and scramble out towards me and nip at my heels. Of course I was sprinting at this time, adrenaline moving me fast so I didn't pause to get a good look. Maybe she had pups, or guarding his lair. This made me take a longer difficult path back, being tired I didn't want to have to out run him. I eventually looked forward to our nightly rendezvous.

Over time he stopped barking and just followed me at a safe distance with a low growl, getting closer to me and traveling almost the entire distance to the center town lights.

I suppose the dog biscuits I brought didn't hurt. He would wait in the shadows for me to return for the run back, never getting too close. I did notice as the weeks past, he wasn't so mangy. In fact he wasn't a dog . . . he was a prairie wolf, a dingo, a coyote, I guess that would explain the howling if I was late.

The night of my experience I ran right by him full gallop not a thought to even drop his biscuits. He knew something wasn't right as he followed, but off the road through the brush.

As my spirit rose into the sky, I did see him cautiously running along, I even saw him stop and look up at me. He followed me with his eyes as I moved off. He could see me or sense my spirit fly off.

I knew it was him even this far from our meeting place, there were no street lights or activity to turn him away.

When I started my limp home he followed. I reached for his biscuits, luckily I had a few broken crumbs to satisfy him. I laid them in a pile and walked on ahead. This seemed to tell him I was alright. Later as I sat by the willow he went a few yards away across the dirt road and made himself comfortable.

I felt safer wondering about the bears, cougars, and wildlife everyone teased me about. At one point I had heard howling in the distance, like a dog pack making its rounds. He let out one short yep . . . and the howling stopped. I felt protected (probably not a good idea). He was nowhere in sight when the old man offered me a ride. Maybe the loud muffler and diesel roar, scared him off. From that day on he would run with me side by side to the edge of town, wait, for up to an hour and run back.

Maybe he was my kindred spirit—maybe my father watching over me, maybe just a mangy mutt looking for a hand out.

Hog-eye day was the end of the summer celebration and had nothing to do with the annual Bushwhacker festival. It was more like a back to school block party. All free just a locals weekend BBQ get together.

Why I had to jog to the phone booth. It was a long-distance call. No cell phones back then. My Uncle's one landline-phone was placed in the living room right outside their bedroom door. No privacy. I also needed the exercise, and night was the best running weather. Once early on, I was pulled over by the police; because there was an 11 pm curfew, I didn't have my license with me . . . Brought to the police station to be bailed out by my annoyed uncle as a character witness . . . I became good friends with the police, and had special privileges to be jogging at night. Long frizzed out hair, (from the odd hard water) . . . and a Charlie Manson beard. A prime suspect running late at night. I did shave after that incident.

I believe it was my father's voice I heard, and him driving the farm truck, or possibly his aura coming through the driver. How did he know where I lived? Did I dream it? Was I hallucinating? Was I home in bed sick the whole time (not running at all)?

I believe it was all true. How or why would I remember a dream after thirty years, so vividly. With such *a huge impact on my life*. . . .

Shat Happened!

A special shout-out to Cousin Charlie, who remained a rock-star by becoming the Head Tennis Pro at a posh country club somewhere in Texas. I am jealous . . .

Cousin Dale who is still drumming in California to this day. Seeing him for the first time since the tour; opened the flood gates.

Cousin Giles, I always wanted to be a big brother.

'Injun Joe' R.I.P.

The mind is a wonderful thing. It has a way of dulling the scary things and slightly padding the outcome of reality. This is my truth, though I know it seems unlikely.

Boo Ya!

Special thanks and recognition to:

My tennis partners: Laurie, Super Dave, Jeffrey Martin, Mike Chwalek, Frank Todesco, Chris Knapp, John Hart, Chuck McStay, Steve Motyka, Mike Friedman, Richie, Daryl.

Teammates: John Panzica, Alfredo, Mike Haynes, John Clifford, Mark Herson, Ernie

The Guys from the Hole:
Dave Malatesta, Nino, Bill and John

Guys from Aylsworth: Mike Bourcier, Marc Corbeil, Russ, Dale, Lance, Frank, and Herman.

The Match point league:
Sue & Steve Nespolo, Ted and Sue, John Salzillo, Gerry and Graham, Chris and Dan Marques, Jerry and Dennis,

The Forecourt crew:
Charlie Michaelman, Bob V . . . the Morins

Mixed teammates:
Sue Martin, Sandy, Karen, Jen, Kevin, Steve, Denise, Gerry, and Lori.

Volleyball teammates: Chris, Chris, Chris, Jimmy, Ellen.

Band mates: Tom, Ski, Newt, Chip and Mike Roy

Basketballers: Leo, Chuck Durang, Chuck Roessler, Greg Murphy, John DeMeo, Wilky, Steve Smith, Mark Cobb, Peter, Jim, Ted, Don, Paul, Doug and Don Dumont,

Family: Mom, Ron, Jan, Delight, Joy, Brock, Chance, Kim, Aubrey, Jayce, Herb and Honey (BB).

The Man, the Myth, the Legend:

I had been writing an article for a tennis magazine about picking the perfect partner and leaving the old sour one. That narrative quickly turned into a tribute for my abandoned partner when he was diagnosed with terminal cancer. We played together that summer with a fresh new attitude about life, becoming the best of friends.

Contemplating how his peers would remember him, I took this opportunity to rewrite the story with him. We laughed and reminisced while he laid bedridden many late nights well past midnight.

When Mike's story was perfected I would bring other stories of our adversaries. It past the time and made him forget his discomfort. It was as if he was back on the tennis court, his sanctuary for the past year.

Mike was the catalyst for this book of short stories. He pushed me to put them in book-form and let the world read them . . . at least our friends. Of course they would get to read about him. To be with him (in spirit) one more time.

His story was written as a recovery story not a death sentence. It was of courage and determination not grief and sorrow. **He was a joy to be around as he soaked in every moment, every warm breeze, every sip of water, every prick of pain.**

I will severely miss him.

In memory of a dear friend, **'Michael Chwalek'**

THE End